50
24

How to Be an Adult
in Faith and Spirituality

David Richo

Paulist Press
New York / Mahwah, NJ

Unless otherwise noted, the scripture quotations outlined herein are from the New Revised Standard Version Bible, copyright © 1989 by the Division of Christian Education of the National Council of Churches of Christ in the U.S.A. Used by permission.

Cover design by Lynn Else
Book design by John Eagleson

Copyright © 2011 by David Richo

All rights reserved. No part of this book may be reproduced or transmitted in any form or by any means, electronic or mechanical, including photocopying, recording or by any information storage and retrieval system without permission in writing from the publisher.

Library of Congress Cataloging-in-Publication Data
Richo, David, 1940–
   How to be an adult in faith and spirituality / David Richo.
     p.   cm.
   Includes bibliographical references.
   ISBN 978-0-8091-4691-8 (alk. paper)
   1. Spiritual formation. 2. Maturation (Psychology)–Religious aspects–Christianity. 3. Psychology, Religious. 4. Christianity–Psychology. I. Title.
   BV4511.R53 2011
   204–dc22   2010054148

Published by Paulist Press
997 Macarthur Boulevard
Mahwah, New Jersey, 07430
www.paulistpress.com

Printed and bound in the
United States of America

With respect for and appreciation of
everyone at Word and Life in Santa Barbara
for all the heartful graces we share
through, with, and in one another

Contents

Introduction

"The religious experience and faith of a mature person gives the most comprehensive and invulnerable security, the largest scope for self-realization possible."

—HARRY GUNTRIP, BRITISH PSYCHOLOGIST
AND METHODIST MINISTER

Before sitting down this morning to work on this manuscript, I walked over to the radio to turn off the news. The last words I heard were: "A *candle*-light *vigil* will be held tonight for the three *fallen* police officers." I thought to myself: "This is an example of folk-religion." Without connection to an institution we use the traditional religious elements of ritual, i.e., candles at night, and a community vigil—a procession in silence and ending in standing at attention. Instead of using the word "dead" the radio announcer used the word "fallen," which has a religio-patriotic connotation.

The voice on the radio is a reminder that most of us cannot help being religious when we face ultimates such as death, especially heroic or tragic death. It is understandable that the elements of religion appear automatically when something happens that creates communal grief or joy. We feel reverently compassionate and we show it by a ritual that helps us move through our experience with a sense of contribution to the community and comfort to ourselves. These are the perennial ways that religion has provided resources for us as we grieve.

In the example above, no religious group set up the vigil or suggested the candles. It was not a church leader who wrote the news bulletin. The human psyche has its own elemental religion. Indeed, our brains seem wired to practice religious rituals and to believe in the transcendent. Even when people are not connected to a church, they naturally invent and perform consoling rituals, especially in or after a crisis. They will refer to this inclination as "spiritual" rather than religious.

Nowadays people often say: "I am spiritual but not religious." Actually, religion and spirituality have coexisted in the human story and have much in common. They do not have to be at odds. They are not dualistic but complementary. Indeed, in the course of history, institutional religion has greatly contributed to personal spirituality. It did this by maintaining its four perennial components: belief, morality, ritual, and devotion. A healthy religion with maturely held beliefs, wise moral values, relevant rituals, and heartfelt devotion can contribute to adult spirituality. Our faith centers around the four components of both of religion and spirituality.

Religion, for instance, can certainly serve as a useful guide to moral uprightness against the shadowy inclination of our species toward greed and aggression. Religious leaders like Gandhi, Martin Luther King Jr., Mother Teresa, Desmond Tutu, and the Dalai Lama have shown us that possibility. Their connection to a religion activated their spirituality and faith.

The four components of religion—belief, morality, ritual, devotion—actually turn out to be the drivers of spirituality also. The main difference is that an institutional religion standardizes the four for everyone, while spirituality designs each of them in accord with individual preferences. Institutional religion is formally organized; spirituality is experiential and personal. If the ceremony for the fallen police officers happened in a formal church ritual, it would be called religious even though it used exactly the same elements as in the spiritual ritual: candles, procession, etc.

Spirituality without formal religion is common nowadays. The four elements of religion evoke a reaction in many adults who have a maturing faith. They want to think for themselves and design *beliefs* based on their experience rather than hold only the beliefs that are sanctioned by an official religious hierarchy. They want to act with *moral* integrity but they trust an inner organismic wisdom over injunctions that impose one set of values on everyone. They want to engage in *rituals* that enact their ever-evolving needs and want to feel *devotion* in accord with what moves their hearts. Mystics throughout the history of all churches were able to maintain these values within a religious context.

Both religion and spirituality can contribute to our evolution as loving and wise humans who are conscious of powers beyond ourselves that assist us in the direction of love and wisdom. When that becomes a focus of our life it is called faith, and it happens when we are religiously oriented or spiritually conscious.

In this book I am proposing that religion can be a useful force in our spiritual growth. Likewise, both religion and spirituality are useful in our psychological growth. Religion refers to a natural inclination and intention in human experience that recognizes a transcendent force in the universe. Religion can also refer to an institution, in which case it can be facilitating or dominating.

A *facilitating* religion helps our faith and spirituality grow to their full stature. Our spirituality will then no longer be a hodge-podge of what is recommended by the new-age movement mixed with smatterings of Asian religions, a fuzzy sense of shamanism, and prevailing rituals. We can develop our spiritual consciousness enormously by gathering the lost treasures that religion has preserved and investing them into our spirituality. This is the act of faith that combines religion and spirituality.

A *dominating* religion, overly institutionalized, focuses on its own survival and advancement. Usually, it works hand in glove with the purposes of the state, e.g., supporting political policies rather than prophetically critiquing them. Such a dominating religion often finds ways to control and repress people. It can be anti-evolutionary, fear-based, or simply feel-good. An adult suspects a religion like that, no matter how secure it may lead her to feel. An adult trusts only what *launches*. She does not focus so much on her own satisfaction that she loses sight of a new horizon.

A facilitating religion opens us to new ways of being human in the context of a historical tradition. Then our faith is a response to the unique riches that religion has gathered over the centuries. The main riches of religion are the archetypes of our deepest psyche, the images that reflect our fullest potential, the ritual styles that reflect mystical awareness, the personal devotion that grants us a sense of an accompanying presence on life's journey, and the sense of meaning in events and experiences that reveal a transcendent glory in being fully human. My intention in this book is to help locate these gifts and show us how to receive them as our true and longed-for legacy. Faith is the link in that wonderful process.

Spirituality without religion loses out on full connection to the ways humans have related to life's mysterious questions over the centuries. Finding meaning in the world and living in accord with it is how our healthy ego develops and how our sense of self grows. By meaning and depth we mean whatever appears as More than what our intellect may report or our desires may describe. Religion is about the More in life, the transcendence of the flat-line world in favor of an invisible reality in and behind all that we see. Faith is how we make contact with that transcendent reality. Spirituality is how we express it.

Of course, one can be a psychologically healthy adult with or without institutional religion. Some sense of the transcendent, however, seems to be a valuable ingredient in our appreciation of our own wholeness. Buddhist author Stephen Batchelor says: "If I deny the presence of something transcendent which can impinge upon and affect me unpredictably, I am bound to reduce spiritual practice to the application of techniques. A spiritual attitude, it seems, must acknowledge something that is both transcendent and active in the world." Perhaps everyone who wants More than what the world ordinarily offers has faith.

This book does not suggest the necessity of joining a religion but does attempt to show the value of using religious resources in the face of life's conflicts. It also focuses on how faith, both as religious and spiritual, can be ways of becoming more richly human. We can bolster our spiritual sense when we claim and include the contributions of religion in our spirituality. A healthy adult will not want to miss out on any of the sources of wisdom in the library of human experience.

In this book we will be exploring how to be an adult in our faith, how to be adult about what we can value in religion and how to be adults who are spiritually aware without being superstitious or superficial. Our topic is about using religious and spiritual resources when we are or are not members of a church.

In the heroic journey model we leave and then return to where we began with a more expanded perspective. To reconnect with what is positive in family, education, and religion is a contribution to the journey. We find the riches in our origins, many or few, and reinvest them for use in our present life. This book is intended to help us with this project.

For some, there is no return to our childhood religion, but there is a discovery of something more or different. That is legitimate too and can mean moving on with no animosity. This book can help us learn to do that.

Adult faith will not include childish dependency but interdependency. The faith that results has power and is empowering, true good news. We are to become as little children according to the Bible but not to *remain* as little children. Our values are nurtured and fed by more and more understanding not of concepts but of our place and purpose in the universe. Then faith is an energy that sustains us in our exploring rather than a tie to one safe set of answers.

Along my own religious journey, I notice three signifi-
cant phases of faith. I can recall that in Catholic high school
I could believe only what aligned exactly with the official
teachings from Rome. In the seminary I expanded my beliefs
but could trust only what was backed up by respected and
liberal theologians. Now I notice a whole new style. I check
out my emerging beliefs with my honored mentors, no longer only Catholic. Perhaps someday only I will decide what I
believe, on my own, though feedback is always appealing to
an adult who wants to remain open.

This book is meant to provide an opportunity to examine our faith, our religious beliefs and memberships, and our
spirituality to see how they align to healthy adult living. Do
our beliefs keep us caught in prejudices or literality? Does
our membership in a church or spiritual community help us
grow in interdependence or keep us dependent?

We can learn how religion and spirituality can foster growth into an adulthood in which we find our identity
in our own way. We might then discover the transcendent
splendors that life and timekeeping offering to us, always in
unique ways, always with bliss-bestowing hands. Those are
the hands that lift us up onto the train that is going where we
need to go. Then faith is trust that this is so. It may include
membership in a religion or not.

Religion will never go away, but only assume new forms.
For instance, we notice that computer science attempts to
offer what religion promises. It does this by providing every
person with a vast virtual world of More that transcends
ordinary human conditions and limitations. The Internet
has the quality of omniscience, a traditional belief about
divine power. It is like religion in how it dictates morality, for
instance, when one feels it is legitimate to download music
under copyright, since it *can* be done so easily on a computer.
It is also most like the unconscious in which there is no past
or future since all is known and doable simultaneously. The
Internet, also like religion, offers community in its intricate

and immediate access to others, like or unlike ourselves. In a way, though, religion also offers virtual community when it suggests that we love those we cannot see.

There are five resources that have helped me find a more adult approach to religious and spiritual faith, all of which will appear in the chapters that follow: modern theological and biblical research, Buddhist practices, mystical theology, archetypal psychology, and evolutionary perspectives.

In modern theology and biblical research we come to understand the origin of our beliefs and find new pathways to into them. In Buddhism we are grounded in the reality of the givens of life with no demand for rescue. In the mystical traditions of all religions we find that God is not a person in the sky but a way of describing the transcendent dimension of all reality, accessible to all and unbrokered by an institution. In the archetypal view, Carl Jung helps us see that religious figures and themes represent the energies in the collective psyche of humanity. In the evolutionary view of Sri Aurobindo and Pierre Teilhard de Chardin, as well as more recently in Ken Wilber, we are realizing that the divine is the future direction in ever-burgeoning consciousness. Science proposes that evolution is driven by chance and necessity. Religion says that evolution is how consciousness and Spirit unfold in time so that the world can move from greed, hate, and illusion to generosity, love, and realism.

We can grow in the holding environment that a spiritually trustworthy religion offers. We cannot grow psychologically if we still cling to childish beliefs or to authority's approval of all that we do. We can also grow without religion at all since not everyone responds to life in that way. In any case, a spiritually bountiful religious tradition can offer valuable gifts that illumine and animate us. Our part is to update our religious tradition into an adult spiritual consciousness. Religion's part is to allow that, to encourage it, and even lead the way.

Since most people find a life purpose that involves becoming more than who they were to begin with, religion can help because it is precisely about the More. In this case, the More is more consciousness, more wisdom, more love. Our faith goal is to activate each of these gifts in our own unique way with the people in our world, in the place where we are, in the time we have—all so precious and poignant. Then the true religion is the one that helps us be true to ourselves and the world is richer for it.

Our awareness of the vastness of our inner life and its eternal purpose is what people of faith have called awareness of the presence of God.

> *"The ascent to the divine life*
> *is the human journey,*
> *the Work of works,*
> *the acceptable Sacrifice.*
> *This alone is humanity's real*
> *business in the world."*
>
> —SRI AUROBINDO, *THE LIFE DIVINE*

Chapter One

Healthy Self, Healthy Beliefs

"God and Nature bid the same."

—JOHN MILTON, *PARADISE LOST*, BOOK VI

Freud regarded the holding of religious belief as a defensive structure in the ego, something that holds us back, rather than something that can help us evolve. Was Freud right when he counseled us to stop being children and face the challenge of life as it is, without the consolations of God and religion? Religion can indeed be an opiate that leads to complacency in the face of life's challenges. It can also prod and encourage us to take action for justice, peace, and love, as saints and heroes have demonstrated so admirably. We see examples of religious motivation in Gandhi, Martin Luther King Jr., Mother Teresa, Desmond Tutu, the Dalai Lama.

A healthy religious faith, like a healthy childhood, offers not an opiate but nurturing and growth-promoting comforts. It balances this with challenges that stretch us. This is how it can include the two essential features of human growth: we need to be held lovingly and yet to walk on our own. We need to be safe at home but also sent off to school. We need a religion that consoles us in personally difficult times and one that pushes us to design a future that will save the planet, no matter what the cost to our own coziness. Facilitating religious voices do counsel in that way. For instance, a facilitating religion can help us make a commitment to integrity, goodness, and love. This takes effect both individually and collectively. It increases our self-esteem and makes the world a better place.

A healthy adult is one who values and maintains soundness of body and sanity of mind. Any program or institution that becomes part of her life will therefore have to facilitate both bodily and mental health. Religion and spirituality are relevant and therefore appealing to adults when they foster these two essential areas of health. Thus a religion that prohibits blood transfusions will not be acceptable to a sound adult. A spirituality that produces inappropriate guilt will not be satisfactory to a sane adult. Faith for an adult can be placed only where religion, spirituality, sanity, and health are all in agreement.

In addition to soundness of body and sanity of mind, we also have the possibility of sanctity of lifestyle. This means acting with moral uprightness, universal love, and enlightened wisdom in daily life. A religious and spiritual tradition that facilitates such sanctity and offers practices that help us advance in it will be welcomed by an adult as a complement to soundness of body and sanity of mind. With all three up and running, we are more than healthy; we are whole.

As we align our psychological work and our spiritual growth in the direction of wholeness, we seek:

> Structures of religion and spirituality that can hold our lively, passionate, and evolving selves

> Perspectives of faith that honor the contributions of all religious and spiritual traditions

> Boundaries of behavior that are free from repression while respectful of limits

> Encouragement of thoughtful and joyful choice rather than fear-based obligation

We have a psychological instinct toward health, in us since childhood. It places the locus of evaluation within ourselves. So when we buy into religious injunctions that contradict our natural instincts, we are overriding our organismic wisdom. For instance, it is a developmental task of puberty to establish our own unique identity. If our religion insists that we should not think for ourselves but, instead, unquestioningly adopt its perspectives, we are following a psychologically unsound principle. In addition there is an element of abuse in severe moral injunctions that shame rather than instruct us. They make us feel isolated, the opposite of the communion that we will walk so long to find and that religions go so far to promise.

Children are told what to do. Adults are *called* to what they are here to do. "Told" is in the realm of obedience. "Being called" is in the realm of faith. Obedience is a useful and necessary convention to let a family run smoothly when we are children and to make a society run smoothly when we are grown up. As examples, we see the value in obeying traffic laws and paying taxes for safety and for the maintenance of an infrastructure. These are adult reasons for obedience. Erich Fromm expressed this idea well: "Man's aim in humanistic religion is to achieve the greatest strength, not the greatest powerlessness; virtue is self-realization, not obedience."

An adult asks: Is this moral rule conducive to health, both physically and psychologically? We are religiously adult when we notice what in our religion fosters our healthy development and what interferes with our well-being and then subscribe accordingly.

Religion is like anything else in our experience. It can be ego-driven or Self-enlivening, egoic or spiritual, facilitating or dominating:

A religion that opposes who we know we are is unacceptable to an adult. A religion that celebrates who we know we are is appealing to an adult.

A religion that keeps us ignorant does not help us evolve. A religion that helps us integrate information from all areas of knowledge helps us evolve.

A religion that keeps us dependent does not help us grow. A religion that launches us into interdependence does help us grow.

A religion that keeps us afraid does not help us love. A religion becomes meaningful when we are not afraid of hell fire but rather on fire with a love that is bigger than any fear we ever had.

Cultural change happens when, no matter what a church says, people just start seeing things differently. They no longer take authority seriously when it has become atavistic. Something becomes so commonplace, for example, living together before marriage, that it can no longer be looked upon by the population as shameful as it was before.

Change can also occur when people laugh at outmoded views. This came through to me one day when I asked a chaplain at a university if he taught the students the old moral view that masturbation was a mortal sin. He said, "Certainly not. If I did they would only laugh at me." Inhumane religious teachings will be seen for what they are and disregarded, especially by the young. Indeed, as adolescents we are meant to explore our bodies freely as a way of knowing ourselves and becoming sexually mature. This interest continues into and throughout adulthood. An institution that outlaws self-pleasuring contradicts that innate wisdom.

Catholic theologian Karl Rahner contrasted the "interior catechism" of the adult to the need for pronouncements from Rome. That "catechism" is our trustworthy inner locus of evaluation. An adult may listen to religious authority but he will follow an authority only if what it says fits with his inner sense of appropriateness. He backs this up with what science and psychology contribute to his knowledge. This is how his faith becomes more adult.

On the other hand, we can lull ourselves into self-centeredness if we do not look for challenges from religion. An adult seeks and achieves balance by listening to himself *and* to traditional sources. We know we are on track when we love more, have more wisdom, and bring more healing to the world. We know we are evolving when we are not as concerned about personal salvation as about co-creating a world of justice, peace, and love.

Our faith aligns with the story of our lives. It has a childhood layer and an adult layer. It passes through phases, like all living realities. I use an example from my own life. My bicycle had no specific problem, but it was certainly not providing a fully satisfactory ride, so I took it to the bike shop. The mechanic looked closely at it and then said: "Your problem is that you have parts from three different eras. You bought some of them when German parts were in vogue, some when Japanese parts were recommended, and some when American parts seemed best. They all work on their own, but not so well together. So you have no specific problem, but you can expect to feel some discomfort and lack of coordination on the bike. The alternative is to remove some parts and update them with replacements that are all the same."

As I left the shop, I suddenly realized that what the mechanic said about my bike applied to my religion too. I have some beliefs from childhood, some from seminary training, and now some from my own discovery of new pathways in mysticism, Jung, Buddhism, and contemporary theology. This may explain why I often feel a discomfort about my own religious life, without seeing anything specific I can fix. And I am not willing to remove anything totally and update in accord with only one perspective.

Many of us began with unambiguous religious views of right and wrong, of life, sex, and death, and of who God is.

Now we are confused because we have lost our neatly organized framework about both this life and the next.

In our psychological life too, we combine childhood, personal experience, and what we have learned from therapy and the self-help movement. They do not match up easily, so we may not feel totally comfortable with our personalities, yet we do survive. We are not willing to scuttle any one of our resources. Our work in adult faith is to integrate the three eras. The result will be a smoother ride on life's journey. We do not have to throw away our past, but we can learn to carry it more comfortably and update it a little at a time, as I am doing with my bicycle—and as I hope to do in this book in the area of religion, spirituality, and faith.

The Power of Childhood

A transitional object, such as a teddy bear, is used by a toddler to remind him of his absent mother. Soon he will find security in himself and will no longer need the symbol. Of course, all through life we may use objects, or even people, to get us through transitions into more independence. The shiny car, the electronic equipment, the cozy relationship may all be ways of finding security externally until it can flourish in ourselves.

Religion happens in the transitional space between what is now and what More can be. In childhood it presents simple ways of understanding the divine. It is psychologically harmless for any interim symbol to be a makeshift bridge until we are ready for a new level of awareness. God as a person in the sky is an example of a transitional object early on life's journey. When we move into a full adult spiritual consciousness, we may see the More not in a supreme being above us but in the being of all beings, that is, in all things. We have a more mystical realization about reality that shows God-as-person to be an approximating metaphor rather than a literal object. Theologian Raimondo

Panikkar asks, "Is not divinity infinite life in eternal participation more than a supreme individual Being?"

Often our representation of God is based on our experience of our parents. Then God is the transitional object we carried into adulthood from childhood, so we could bring our parents with us as we simultaneously became independent. Such a transference from our past is meant to be let go of in favor of an experience of the divine that happens in the present and is free from parental images. That is the adult transition into a healthy religious consciousness. *If I love my parents/religion now, they were the right ones for me?*

Returning to religion in old age because of a fear of death is another example of clinging to a transitional object, this time, the big transition.

Early religious teachings remain in our psyche for a lifetime if the bond was strong to begin with. We may then dispense with religious beliefs, even turn against them, but they sit inside waiting for the right time and place to reemerge. If the bond to our religion was minimal and religious teachings never really took hold, this is, of course, less likely. The seed that fell on shallow ground can be swept away by winds of change. The seed absorbed deep into the earth keeps sprouting at unexpected times.

Our transitions in religion are like the ones in our evolution from childhood to adulthood: The infant takes; the adult has learned to give. The child seeks ways to escape fear; the adult has found ways to love fearlessly. The immature person uses coercion to get his way; the mature person learns to cooperate. The person whose mind is undeveloped has blind obedience; the grownup in mind has freedom of thought and remains open to information from a variety of sources.

In childhood faith we ask God to give us what we want; the adult asks only to be generous. A childish faith is driven by a fear of hell; an adult by love. The immature person may force his beliefs on others; the mature person tries to form cooperative bonds with people of all faiths. Blind obedience is not in the vocabulary of an adult in faith, only freedom to explore and openness to manifold voices.

Finally, a psychological question arises: What is the difference between psychotic ideation and religious beliefs? How is believing there is a God who loves us different from believing we are Napoleon? There are three main differences: In a psychosis, the information is coming from inside one's own head, not as teachings from a long ancestry of honored masters. Second, having religious beliefs allows for a functional life, but that is not possible while being psychotic. To believe that God judges us does not render anyone dysfunctional; someone believing that he is God the Judge does. Third, the psychotic beliefs lead to dangerous, bizarre, or compulsive behavior while mature religious beliefs do not.

Stages of Growth and Faith

> *"Can you tell me how to grow? Or is it*
> *unconveyed, like melody or witchcraft?"*
>
> —LETTER FROM EMILY DICKINSON
> TO THOMAS HIGGINSON, 1862

As consciousness evolves through a spectrum so does our sense of mental health as well as our ways of being religious. To say that faith is living means that it can grow, the way our bodies and minds do. A living faith cannot remain the same throughout our life span. Each stage of life is a new challenge to be ourselves and to be with others, to be individuals and to be connected, to be at home and to be in the world. All this has to happen in ever new ways. Change is built into our development, and how ironic that we fear it so much.

As we have been noticing, the path to healthy psychological living is a heroic journey. The phases of our religious experience may also mirror those of the heroic journey:

We are contained in a familiar set of beliefs and values that we learned from our family and religious teachers. This phase gives us security.

We step out of our safe container and question our beliefs. This can represent a "loss of faith" or be a phase in the evolution of our faith. This phase brings up doubt.

We come back to our roots with new appreciation, or we come back with a whole new perspective. This phase is our adult achievement.

We begin in the comfort of belonging, move to an alienation, and finally integrate our experience with our beliefs in our own unique way.

Normal development means moving from phase to phase.

Regression or fanaticism result when we become fixated in the containment phase.

Fixation in the doubt phase leads to problems with authority.

Faith also moves through stages like these:

Stage One: We take teachings literally.

Stage Two: We appreciate the teachings as symbolic and metaphorical, not as literal.

Stage Three: We accept paradox and mystery as inherent in human existence and in spiritual consciousness and give up seeking final explanations.

We also notice the levels of human development in the three phases of childhood development. They are the same phases that might characterize adult intimacy. First, we ask to be understood by someone who cares for us, to be mirrored, loved, held, comforted. Then we imitate the other because we admire her. We accept the challenge to change into being more than we were by expanding our personalities to reflect some of her positive features. Finally, we become peers in community with the other, equal in competence and in powers of self-nurturance.

We see those same phases in Twelve-Step programs, acceptance by the group, imitation of the group, being one of the group that helps newcomers.

Likewise in religion, we begin with the sense that God loves us as we are. We then imitate the devotion of sages and saints. We finally see God as a personification of who we are in our higher Self. In this way, the three phases of our development as persons are the same as growth in faith.

Auditing Our Religion

> *"I have sworn upon the altar of God an eternal hostility against every form of tyranny over the mind of man."*
>
> —THOMAS JEFFERSON IN A LETTER
> TO DR. BENJAMIN RUSH, 1800

Religions have a story that believers are meant to reenact, for instance, sharing communion as Christ did at the last supper or sitting meditatively as Buddha sat. The story a religion offers seems to fit just right when it is about love, wisdom, and healing not only among individuals but as commitments to the evolving of the planet. It comes across as dissonant when it is about the opposite: hate, ignorance, and division, especially in a parochial way. A healthy religion promotes love that is universal, wisdom that is found in all traditions, and healing that reconciles individual people and nations too.

A religion whose story is that God wants everyone to be concerned only about her near and dear will not sound quite right to a fully conscious and compassionate adult. It will become irrelevant to humanist liberal thinkers when it prohibits freedom, especially in acting in accord with one's natural instincts, e.g., acting on one's sexual orientation or living together outside marriage.

We need an evaluative tool to tell which story makes sense to each of us. That tool can be what leads to universal and unconditional love, the wisdom of the ages, and healing power. These are the qualities that are respected in all traditions and throughout all of history. They help us evaluate whether our religion really works.

We might look at our religious models and teachers and expect them to be living exemplars of the veracity of the teachings. An adult knows that the teachings are the teacher. The lifestyle of the teacher is a comment only on that individual, not on the tradition he represents. Mature adults will be saddened by hypocrisy in their teachers, but they will not lose their faith because of it.

The *literal* facticity of the story is necessary in fundamentalist religions. This view does not allow for the bigness of truth that transcends fact, what literally happened, in favor of a larger *metaphorical* meaning. This does not mean that some religious events did not really happen but rather that they are meant to be seen as happenings that are still in evidence in our lives today.

We may confuse fact and truth when we limit truth to fact. Literalism about the Bible is recent in history. It began as a reaction to the theory of evolution from Charles Darwin in *Origin of Species* in 1858. At that time, the creation story in Genesis was taken literally, so scientific theory or evidence to the contrary was considered an attack against faith.

A religion with all the answers may fall prey to the admonition of Abraham Maslow, who wrote, "Most people lose or forget the subjectively religious experience, and redefine religion as a set of habits, behaviors, dogmas, and forms which, at the extreme, becomes entirely legalistic and bureaucratic, conventional, empty, and in the truest meaning of the word, anti-religious." This statement is reminiscent of Allen Ginsberg's pithy statement: "Absolutes are coercion."

A good poem leaves us with unanswered questions. Then we find room for our central ineradicable and universal human longing, the journey toward personal meaning. A religion that is suspicious of pilgrim journeyers will not appeal to adults on such a venture. An adult looks to a religion that does not explain reality since that is a closing. An adult seeks a religion that illuminates reality because that is an opening. Faith is always about opening.

Religions that are healthy do not tie an individual to one way but offer variety to their devotees. In the *Bhagavad-Gita* (4:11) we hear Krishna, the Hindu god of love, say, "In whatever way people come to me, even so do I accept them. Whatever path they choose is mine." In our Western tradition we hear Sir Gawain in the *Quest for the Holy Grail*, "Let us set forth to behold the Grail unveiled." The knights "thought it a disgrace to go forth [in the same direction]. Each entered the forest at a point that *he himself had selected*, where it was darkest and *where there was no way or path*." To be individual is to seek our own path into life's mystery.

Spirituality can be individual or connected to a community. Religion, as we are using the word here, is connected to an institution or community. As adults we want to examine that institution before we commit ourselves to it. To provide a healthy context for an adult, a religion cannot be authoritarian. It has to honor our rights and needs. We may not know the full extent of a religious tradition, however, if our only experience of it is parochial or local.

For instance, our appreciation of the power of education cannot kick in easily if all we have to go on is our experience in grammar school. Then we might believe that school means sitting up straight, walking in line, and swallowing whole whatever the teacher presents. Only in college do we notice the bigness that education can have. We notice that we can sit in any position, that we can question our teachers and propose an alternative to what they propose to us as long as we can make a reasonable defense for our views. Now we see that education can be an adult-making experience. In grammar school it was kept in a childhood mode. In college it is in the adult mode. We do not then turn against our early education but only expand on it.

This applies to religion. We can look for ways to find what is useful in our religious past and integrate it into our present experience. We do this best when we are introduced to the "college" version. As an example I can recall an experience from my own life. All I knew of Catholicism was what I learned in catechism class at St. Patrick's Church and in St. Mary's Catholic High School. My religion was small, containing rigid formulations of beliefs, some superstitions, a narrow morality emphasizing mostly sexual repression, and many prejudices—none of which was allowed to be debated, only accepted.

In my early twenties, I traveled in France and spent a day at a Catholic organization called Pax Christi. The members were mostly people around my age, and I noticed their commitment to nonviolence and to a morality that went beyond the personal into the communal. This was new to me as was the joy in their faces, the free spirit in their manner. They were firmly Catholic but not tied to a rigid orthodoxy or to narrow and repressive moral strictures. For the first time, I realized that Catholicism could have an expansive liberality that can appeal to and accommodate an adult consciousness.

This experience expanded and transcended what I had found at St. Patrick's Church or St. Mary's High School. Here was a universal consciousness, and its bigness showed in the bright faces of the French students I was so happy to be among. That was my first experience of the full-size version of my religion with a cosmic Christ.

Later, I saw it in many more places, for instance in the Catholic presence in the antiwar movement. Without that introduction to what Catholicism could be, I would have believed it could be only the narrow confining religion of my childhood. So now when I assess my religious affiliation, I can judge by more than a catechism class and voices that were telling me not to go too far. Catholicism is also Pax Christi, the Catholic Worker, Dorothy Day, Thomas Merton, Mother Teresa, and more.

We can summarize four prevalent views about religion:

Parochial/Fundamentalist View: Our religion/sect is the only true one and our beliefs were revealed by God to us. There are not many legitimate religions but only one. The rest are approximations, misinterpretations, or simulations.

Reductionist View: Religion is a human invention to control people who are ignorant of science.

Archetypal/Integral View: Religion is a response to the sacred and a way of preserving the deepest truths about who we really are and how we can transform the world.

Cosmic/Universal View: Religion is useful when it opens us to consciousness of our evolutionary destiny to become universal humans who see the bigness of the human journey and its vast implications for the survival of the planet rather than only for individuals who strive for their own salvation.

Pondering the Criteria of an Adult Religion

Here are some characteristics of a religion or religious community that respects us as adults and launches us to become more spiritually aware. Notice that the criteria apply to other areas of life too, e.g., school, job, relationship. Ask yourself if the religion you now espouse fits these adult standards.

Consider these criteria to see if they match your own ideas of a healthy religion and if your own present religion fits them:

> Our religion helps us face the givens of life rather than exempts us from them or guarantees the intervention of a rescuer God on our behalf.
>
> It recommends only what is in keeping with healthy development, physically, psychologically, and emotionally.
>
> It recognizes our right to happiness and its value in human growth rather than insisting that we gain merit by enduring pain, especially in relationships.
>
> It does not take away even one of our basic human rights but rather it guarantees freedom of intellect, imagination, and choice, never demanding that we forfeit them in order to maintain a membership in good standing.
>
> It motivates us to act with universal kindness and personal goodness, not because of fear, guilt, or superstition but because of the love that it affirms to be present in all of us.
>
> It trusts our ability to explore theology without having to adhere to rigid "orthodox" formulations of beliefs.
>
> It does not declare itself to be the "only true way," nor that all truth is in any one book, nor that beliefs be taken literally, but respects the best modern contributions to adult understanding as made by a variety of religious, philosophical, and scientific sources.
>
> It is not prejudiced toward nor militant against others by reason of gender, creed, sexual orientation, race, or political persuasion.

It is joyous and comforting without being separatist, not offering the attitude of "us against the world" but providing a holding environment that grants a sense of belonging, no matter how eccentric our viewpoint—or we—may be.

Its comforts, challenges, and teachings continually move us toward achieving our full stature as rational and concerned adults.

It expands our conscience so that, with increased awareness of global suffering and of ecological issues, we become engaged and make a commitment to personal and political action that promotes justice, peace, and love.

Our childhood religion may not have been geared toward helping us be more adult. Some of our present psychological self-negations may be traceable to our religious past. Our practice is not simply to cancel them. It is important to reframe them to preserve whatever valuable kernel may be found in them:

I am unable to face the givens of life alone.

This becomes: I face the givens of my life and ask for support from those I trust. I also feel myself accompanied by a guiding force that is ever present to assist me in saying yes to what is.

I cannot trust my feelings, my sexuality, my body, or my impulses.

This becomes: I appreciate how my impulses free up my creativity, and I continue to set limits on my impulses when they hurt me or others or when they deter me from my life purpose.

It is dangerous to trust my inner voice rather than the pronouncements of authority.

This becomes: I trust my inner voice and remain open to the suggestions of others especially those with knowledge and experience beyond my own.

My purpose in life is to endure pain, not to be happy.

This becomes: My life purpose is to be as happy as possible and to tolerate the suffering that is natural to me as a human being while doing all I can to alleviate the suffering of myself and others in the world around me.

Chapter Two

What Is Religion?

*"If our religion is based on salvation, our
chief emotions will be fear and trembling.
If our religion is based on wonder, our
chief emotion will be gratitude."*

—CARL JUNG

Religion, like spirituality, affirms that there is More to reality than can be fully known, a transcendent dimension in the world and its history and a transcendent force or Being behind it all. Since transcendence is not visible, faith is required, a belief that there is meaning in life beyond what the mind can know or the eye can see and a trust that we are being held by a providential energy.

In some religious traditions the natural world is only a vestibule to another world where redemption and meaning will happen. William James, in *The Varieties of Religious Experience*, sees this faith as "the bare assurance that this natural order is not ultimate but a mere sign or vision . . . of a many-storied universe, in which spiritual forces have the last word." He wonders if the universal inner need for the transcendent may mean that indeed there is one. James affirms that to live religiously is certainly "to act as if the invisible world were real." *Our longing cannot guarantee the reality of a kingdom of love but our behavior can help it happen.*

Religion is considered by some to be provisional, providing explanations that science is not yet ready to discover.

In materialist science only the tangible is real. This William James calls "agnostic positivism," since then truth can depend only on sense evidence.

Synchronicity, meaningful coincidence, shows that things can happen to us in mysterious and unexplainable ways, certainly beyond our control. This is another example of transcendence. Synchronicity shows that meaning is not simply intra-subjective. Something is at play to move us along on a path. Synchronicity, since it is beyond our control, points to a realm beyond our grasp, effort, or jurisdiction.

The scientific materialist sees a pearl and declares that it is nothing but concentric layers of calcium carbonate in crystalline form. A spiritually oriented person proclaims it to be a symbol of the higher Self. This is indeed a projection. But the scientist who says a pearl is just a pearl is certainly projecting too. He is projecting his belief in a totally flatland world. He is projecting his despair about the More than can be, a grim bias toward vacuity and meaninglessness in life and nature.

Since meaning is ultimately a mystery, we cannot know for certain whether it exists in any objective way, that is, in ways that can be tested by the tools of logic and science. But we do know this: We are more functional in the world and more joyous when we believe that there is meaning. In that sense, we might say that meaning is real operatively, whether or not we are certain it is ontologically real. In a wider more generous sense, meaning is happening whenever we find an opportunity in our predicament to fulfill ourselves, find wisdom, and love more.

For William James religions are basically alike in the ways they report experience of the sacred, the path they offer to transformation, and the moral behavior they recommend, for example, the golden rule. The differences among religious people are in their specific beliefs more than in their general view of reality or morality. Huston Smith wrote that the "primordial tradition" is the same in all religious views:

Reality is more than what we see and we are more than what we think ourselves to be.

Religion proposes that supernatural mysterious forces that transcend nature and can suspend its laws may, at times, influence history through miraculous interventions. These are similar in most traditions: liberation from oppression, arrival of a savior, escape from menace, salvation from a massive flood, frequent outwitting of the forces of evil, healings, etc. They are primal events in religious history that are celebrated in rituals and religious holidays.

Religion usually offers compensation for what cannot be found or trusted in the ordinary world. Each of the givens of life is expanded to include a promise of More in a world beyond this one:

> Here on earth all is impermanent, but heaven is eternal.

> Our plans may go awry, but the divine plan is always in place.

> Things are not fair here on earth, but at the heavenly judgment justice will prevail.

> Suffering is part of life but grants us redemptive merit if we endure it.

> People are not always loving, but God is love unending.

An adult faith is an unconditional yes to the givens of life with a commitment attached to each one:

> Here on earth all is impermanent, but we are nonetheless passionately committed to the predicaments in the human venture and the thriving of the natural world.

> Our plans may go awry, but synchronicity keeps happening, surprising combinations of choice and chance that bring meaning to life events and confirm that our

life is about growth through unexpected circumstances and transitions.

Things are not fair here on earth, but we can fight for justice and we will prevail in some way although not always immediately.

Suffering is part of life, but we do not have to cause suffering. We do not have to stay in situations that cause us suffering. We can grow in character and compassion when we bear suffering that cannot be avoided.

People are not always loving but we can commit ourselves to love, which is how God is love in this moment of time.

Four Elements

As we saw above, religion in all traditions has four main components:

Beliefs that flow from a central affirmation of something/someone transcendent.

Moral values reflected in commandments or precepts.

Rituals in the form of prayer and ceremonies.

Devotion to something or someone transcendent, usually shown as relationship to a divine being.

We show our commitment to traditional religion in our faith response to these four characteristics:

We assent to beliefs.

We live in conscientious commitment to moral values.

We participate in community rituals.

We show devotion by fostering a personal relationship to God.

The four elements of religion are not adventitious or foreign to the human psyche. They coincide exactly with the four main features of a human person:

Our intellect, by imagination, can accommodate beliefs that transcend scientific proof.

Our will can make moral choices.

We enact consciousness in action in the form of rituals.

Our emotions are enlisted in our devotion.

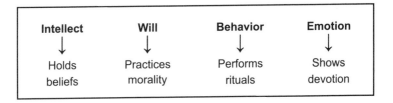

Intellect	Will	Behavior	Emotion
↓	↓	↓	↓
Holds beliefs	Practices morality	Performs rituals	Shows devotion

Healthy adults can thus be religious because the four components of religion and spirituality are all in keeping with the full experience of being human. A spiritually alive religion is not about repression and marching to the same drum. It is immensely liberating since it focuses our natural instincts in ways that activate our best potentials and make us contributors to our fellow humans. Each of the elements is then a cause of happiness:

Our beliefs are meant to be good news of hope for us and all humanity.

Our morality is meant to help us expand our conscience so our love can reach out to all people and nature too.

Our rituals are meant to initiate and celebrate our transitions along life's journey.

Our devotion evokes inner serenity and the joy of feeling loved by powers beyond ourselves.

Healthy adults have some very specific ways of dealing with each element. Here we see clearly that the four components of religion apply to spirituality too:

Regarding *belief,* adults think for themselves but are open to the wisdom of others. Adults with faith will not design their beliefs on the basis of what an authority declares unless it matches and upholds personal experience or an intuitive sense of rightness. Adults are aware nonetheless that they do not have knowledge in areas requiring special training. They will consult the authorities that have proven themselves competent. For instance, we can learn from a capable dentist about dental care, information we do not have on our own. When it comes to that which is a mystery to anyone, however, adults learn mainly from their own experience.

Adults engage in practices of *morality* based on the common opinion of humankind regarding right and wrong. They are careful not to let themselves be influenced by authorities that are coercive, inhumane, or not in keeping with psychological and physical health. Adults will not adhere to moral teachings, for instance, that are based on medieval views about the purposes of the human body or of sexuality. They are careful not to turn to churches that support the state when it comes to forming a conscientious view about participation in war, injustice, or greed.

Religion has preserved the value of *rituals.* Adults perform rituals that make sense to them. They also appreciate the traditional rituals of religion when they are meaningful to them. Adults with faith are not afraid to establish their own rites and rituals to access graces, special powers of goodness, wisdom, or healing. Adults have noticed that grace is everywhere and they participate in the rituals that enact that truth.

Adults are not afraid of emotions and can show *devotedness* to those whom they respect. With faith, they have deep devotion to powers that transcend the finite and look for points of contact. That contact *becomes and feels like a personal relationship*. It seems that all mammals show some form of devotedness. Pets are a supreme example. This devotion seems to be biologically intrinsic to us rather than imposed by religion.

Each of the four components of religion and spirituality is certainly manifest in diverse ways:

One can *believe literally* that religious doctrines originated in a revelation inspired by a transcendent source. One can also believe that the doctrines that the founder of a religion expressed are to be taken metaphorically as a description of the human journey and its transcendent possibilities. The heroic journey motif is then not about someone to admire but about who we are. Religious icons serve a similar purpose. They are mirrors of us at our best.

Some view *morality* as confined to personal sins of omission or commission. Others emphasize collective sin and social consciousness. They might then have a personal mission to right wrongs or to heal divisions among people in the wider world. Morality becomes dangerous when it turns into judgment of those who act differently from ourselves. Then we feel justified in hurting or excluding them, and morality has become an excuse for hate and abuse.

Rituals can mean going through the motions and can become rote. It is also possible to experience rituals as life-sustaining or life-changing. A religiously conscious adult designs rituals that enact a consciousness higher than any ego can construe. The rituals in a church will be especially appealing to adults with an evolutionary consciousness when they notice how participation in them awakens them to social consciousness.

Many of us were indoctrinated about religion in childhood. What was input into us were only the first three components of religion: dogmas, moral teachings about good and evil, and the importance of rituals, including scripture reading. The fourth element, *devotion*, might have been overlooked. It refers to the personal, relational dimension of religion. It also includes imitation, e.g., being like Christ or Buddha in our dealings with others. It is nourished in many ways, including but not limited to intimate prayer, admiration of saints, the use of sensuous metaphors such as God as the Beloved, attention to images, the natural world, the design of the universe.

Most of us were exposed to devotion in traditional forms but were not shown specific styles of imitation. For instance, we may have been indoctrinated in creedal beliefs but not in how to become nonviolent, universal in our compassion, and free from bias toward other religions—all ways of imitating the founder of our religion and the saints who followed him.

The track record of religion in history is not the best. But that record refers to religion as dominating through patriarchy and institutionalism. The possibilities in a facilitating religion are appealing to those who want to take every clue that humanity has given about human wholeness. The four elements are four central clues.

How the four components of religion are to be expressed is usually considered by a church to be revealed by God. Thus *what* to believe, *how* to act morally, *which* rituals to perform, *how* to show devotion are carefully prescribed. Revelation usually refers to scripture, the pronouncements of institutional authority, and historical tradition.

If the relationship of divine *to* human is reframed as reaching the divine *within* the human, then revelation may be about the future, not only the past. It can be mediated through nature, the archetypes of the human psyche, the history of human realizations about the divine, evolutionary consciousness, or mystical realizations directly felt and grasped in interior awareness and experience. In this regard, theologian Raimondo Panikkar writes: "It is certain that no book can constitute the ultimate foundation of any faith, since it is precisely faith that is needed in order to give the book the value of witness." Yet in a strictly fundamentalist view, the Bible is the only legitimate and inspired path to truth. This limits the divine voice to a specific interval in time. Further, since the writers of the Bible were exclusively male, it eliminates women from inspiration.

Religions differ in how they view truth-as-revealed. In *exclusivism* there is only one objective truth and only one true religion that preserves it. In *inclusivism* there is some truth in all religions but these truths are only preparations for and a foreshadowing of the full truth that is found, ultimately, only in one religion. Finally, in *universalism* truth emerges from the ongoing dialogue of all religious and philosophical traditions. In this view, revelation is not limited to a single configuration of truth but a continual revelation throughout time with ever-changing formulations that have to make sense to each new generation. No single church has a stranglehold on this kind of truth. Faith, from this perspective, is a relationship to the divine, and beliefs are ever more recognizable symbols through which faith is manifest. *Do I believe because of what they say* or *do they say what I believe*?

It is hard to imagine religion as nonsectarian, transtraditional, truly universal—while honoring unique contributions too. In a universalistic view, truth is pluralistic, ever-restating itself and ever-evolving. It cannot be pinned to any one statement, formulation, doctrine, dogma, or concept. This kind of truth is a moving reality. Then revelation is a happening that keeps happening in us. Adults will find the universalist view most appealing.

Religion gives life a framework. Some of us need that to be provided to us ready-made through clear declarations and within a specific community setting. Others of us find or construct a framework on our own. It is possible to be religious—to include the four elements of religion and spirituality in our lifestyle—but not be part of any church. We may not be members of a church but be part of a socially conscious community or a Twelve-Step program.

Early Religion

Primitive peoples lived in a world that *presumed* an alternative meaning to the given one. They acknowledged a transcendent reality behind appearances. They observed moral folkways, performed rituals, and showed devotion to their multiple gods. The four elements in religion were present in their lives on a daily basis. In fact, there was no distinction between the spiritual and the material world, the sacred and the profane.

Oppressed and enslaved peoples had a hopeful belief in a mirror universe. In that other world rank, status, and hierarchy are all reversed. The lower the social class the more strongly was religion associated with a promise of salvation or hope for a savior. The Hebrew slaves in Egypt believed that God would someday liberate them. Likewise, the early Christians believed fervently in a parallel kingdom that defied and abrogated the Roman empire and all its power. In the apocalyptic kingdom, God was trusted fully to approve the unapproved and the last were to become first. This is the apocalyptic vision of a future in which goodness and justice will triumph over evil. Here the persecuted will inherit the kingdom. The world's values, for the ancients as for modern religious people, will be justice, peace, and love rather than inequality, war, and hate.

Annual planting among ancient peoples began with ritual prayer that recalled how the gods performed this same task at the beginning of time. The human lifecycle became a repetition of a primal religious event. Whatever happened every year became a promise in perpetuity. Thereby the phases of life and the seasons were believed to exist in a spiritual framework ritualized in a liturgical cycle of celebration.

Among ancient peoples this fostered a sense of belonging here on earth. Repetition and participation give people a sense of rootedness and continuity: "I am real because I am part of something. I have a grander meaning than can be guessed by my mortal body."

In our contemporary world we do not all have conscious beliefs like this. But the collective unconscious maintains a library of myth and symbol that can reconnect us with our origins. In the Jungian perspective, the psyche is a source, not simply a depository of knowledge. We can look within and find revelations about what the world is really about and who we are in it. This reflects the ancient views, including those of later Gnostics and alchemists. The continuity includes and culminates now in our contemporary evolutionary consciousness that aligns the ancient realizations with our new cosmology.

Surviving in our psyche is an "archaic thirst for being," according to Mircea Eliade. This is how humans *require* meaning. Psychologically, it is a need to trust that we are supported by powers that nurture us in our life pursuits and understand us compassionately. Our modern egos may balk at this. They often drive us to want autonomy and independence at the cost of connection. Actually, however, the ego does not have the ability to sustain itself independently. In addition, and ironically, the neurotic ego fears independence and true freedom. With independence it would lose its entitlement to be taken care of. With freedom it would lose its escape hatch of blaming others for what goes wrong. We are often searching for and demanding impossible contradictories.

For the ancient Greeks, the gods did not transcend the natural order. Nor did they fully intervene in human affairs but rather participated in them. Divine interventions worked through human choices and actions. The divine entry into time happened as a form of synchronicity, a sudden insight or deed of valor that happened just in time to save the day.

The insights and deeds were all consistently acknowledged as graces of the gods. Yet the graces were granted only when humans joined in with effort, virtuous determination, and gratitude. We can see how the gods became metaphors for the graces that expand human powers.

As society becomes more complex, the lines between clergy and laity, sacred and profane, are more sharply drawn. This is not so in primitive religion:

> Rituals were meant to show and forge the merging of humanity and God.

> The accent in worship was on identification, participation, and the acting out of archetypal paradigms.

> The world was thought to be renewed annually to recover the sacredness of the original creation.

> In totemism people honored an animal as a companion, guide, friend, helper.

> There was a sense of symbiosis with nature, e.g., a hunter was not simply seeking food but journeying toward a goal, life's quest for truth about who he was and what his relationship to nature entailed.

> The sacred was not connected exclusively to gods. Nature was considered holy too.

> The world of appearances was an epiphany, that is, transparent to a divine Source and Upholder.

> A shaman/healer was trusted as able to see the spirit world directly. His mission often began with a severe trauma or wound in childhood, which he healed on his own. Thereafter the cosmic powers were at his disposal. He could heal others, hide in plain sight, bifurcate, levitate, see more deeply into what was happening in the moment, foretell the future. To the primitive mind, only

the shaman was an individual person. Other people had only a tribal identity. This meant that an afterlife was not considered to be about individual identity but about ongoing participation in the survival of the tribe.

Some beliefs have appeared repeatedly in most early religions. They probably represent the collective truths of our higher Self. These archetypal beliefs provided a context for Christianity as we know it. Here are examples:

Gods can and do become human, incarnate themselves.

Some humans are born from gods or goddesses by virgin birth.

Gods sometimes pay a penalty that humans have incurred.

Gods can give humans their own bodies as spiritual food.

Gods can die and be resurrected.

Some humans can perform miracles, thanks to the help of the gods.

Gods are pleased by pilgrimages to shrines where healing may happen.

Gods are worshiped in special buildings and in liturgies.

Gods respond to rituals, offerings, and prayer from individuals or groups.

Specific gods are patrons for specific purposes and can be prayed to for help in the fulfillment of specific needs.

Gods sometimes are manifest in nature either in special places, e.g., water, fire, or in natural events, e.g., thunder, floods, earthquakes, rainbows.

Gods can see all, know all, and have power over all.

Gods can be triune, three in one.

Gods judge human behavior, and they reward and punish people both here and in a life after death.

The heaven or abode of gods is above earth, and the hell realm is below it. These are associated with reward and punishment.

Those who have died may need the help of prayers, offerings, and rituals by those still on earth.

Those who have died and entered fulfillment can now help the living. Thus humans who have died can be called upon as guides and protectors.

Gods cannot be looked at or known fully by humans while on this mortal plane.

Gods, in disguise or in light, can appear to people and bring useful messages both in waking life and in dreams.

Certain people are graced with special knowledge about how to access divine favor or revelation and perform rituals that grant it.

Myths are not about what really happened in the world of fact but about what always happens in spiritual consciousness or in a parallel universe.

There is no separation between the spiritual and material realms of reality.

Sometimes gods need to be propitiated or we are required to make reparation to them.

Gods care about us and help us fulfill the destiny they designed for us.

The Religion of Patriotism

The ancient Romans feared the gods more than they loved them. The purpose of their religious rituals was to propitiate or petition them for intervention during crises, such as famine or war. The gods were on their side but required reverence from humans to remain so. Religion entirely supported the purposes of the empire: victory in battle, expansion of jurisdiction, prosperity, and high living for the aristocracy.

Our loyalty to religion increases exponentially when it becomes connected to a group experience that grants security and a sense of belonging. Patriotic feeling provides this within a nation. Patriotic ideals and beliefs are drilled into us in grade school. As with religion we imbibe these beliefs before we have a fully critical sense. As children we swallow beliefs whole and without question, no matter what the source of them, no matter how inaccurate, limited, or limiting they may be. We might ever after confuse religion and national loyalty, especially since patriotism offers the same comfort and sense of belonging that we find in religion. I recall in childhood at our parish church how on one side of the sanctuary was the American flag and on the other side was the Catholic flag.

We are stirred to a form of *religious* feeling by patriotic anthems, especially at sports events. Anthems are devotional hymns to the state. "America the Beautiful" is not a travelogue but just such a hymn. Memorial Day, Presidents' Day, Armistice Day, and other holidays are the equivalent of religious holy days. Revelation comes to us in the Declaration of Independence and other cherished documents. The moral teachings are in the Constitution and in the exemplary lives of the founding fathers. The temples are Mount Rushmore, the Jefferson and Lincoln memorials, and local monuments. The rituals are the presidential oaths taken on the Bible, the anthems at sports events, the placing of the wreath at the tomb of the unknown soldier, and so forth. Thus all four elements of religion are included in patriotism. We were even encouraged to show devotion by dying for our country, as we were meant to do for our faith, should the need arise.

Our adult task is not only to form a mature religious consciousness but to learn to have a grown-up patriotism. In medieval times, people were loyal to their lords in an unquestioning way. If that is how we are patriotic now, we are not grown up in that area. Adults can choose to be loyal but not blindly obedient. They can declare that the emperor has no clothes, when necessary.

Healthy adult patriotism is fidelity to one's homeland with keen interest in *and* questioning of its policies. It is not tribal self-interest with a lack of concern for the welfare of other nations. The common good becomes the good of all humanity. Fair trade, social justice, the arts of peace are how it is demonstrated. Spiritually conscious adult patriotism is a pledge of allegiance to policies and practices that further justice, peace, and love, the kingdom described by the founders of most religions—not those of empires.

Conversion to such a spiritual faith is acting in accord with a moral code such as is found in the Sermon on the Mount, in Sufi mysticism, in the Buddhist practice of loving-kindness. The recommendations in those teachings go beyond the ten commandments and are fervently opposed to a corporate greed/war economy.

Patriots with faith refuse collaboration with the establishment and the perpetuating of its values. This means no longer supporting war, torture, retaliation, unfair laws, curtailed rights for minorities, and oppression in any form. An adult with conscientious integrity will not be attracted to a religion that simply mimics and upholds the values of a political system. He will pay attention to the prophetic voice and witness by which religion offers moral alternatives. An individual spirituality does not usually offer that voice but religion does if we listen closely enough, and we can always be the voice too.

The established congregations, Catholic, Protestant, and Jewish, too often do what the religions of ancient Rome did: they support the policies of the state. At the official level, for example, when there have been wars, they did not counsel their young men to refuse to go; they supported induction as a patriotic duty and thereby sanctioned the legitimacy of war. Only a few religious denominations, for example, Quaker, Mennonite, and Amish, take a firm and united conscientious enduring stand against war.

Nonetheless, it is certainly a sign of hope that within all the major congregations there are groups that speak up for nonviolence and human freedom, though usually in the minority. In these days of easy communication, their prophetic voices are not snuffed out. So far in the history of humanity it has been only such marginal religious groups that have made a full commitment to nonviolent resistance to evil. Our evolution will not advance as long as that is the case. The only question is: Which will happen first, an embrace of nonviolence or the destruction of the world?

We can make the political system and the churches into active agents of change by empowering ordinary people and promoting new social movements, changing the assumptions of those with power and changing power itself in ways that make a better life possible for all. Such a commitment is religious since it is about moving toward the More than what is. Olivier de Fontagne, S.J., wrote: "Political involvement conceived as service to the community is a noble task . . . a way of serving others while working to establish a well-balanced church-state relationship." In this perspective, knowledge of God is not limited to theology but in how God is love and how we can love too. In Jeremiah, we hear God referring to Shallum, son of Josiah: "He judged the cause of the poor and needy; then it was well. 'Is not this to know me?' says the Lord" (22:16).

Religion in America is often feel-good rather than life-changing. Religion, not God as love, is then the object of belief. Compare using religion to support the status quo with Ernst Renan's description of the person of faith as "torn with discontent and possessed with a passionate thirst for the future." That future is the real godliness.

Finally, it is important to acknowledge that not only political liberals are adult. A politically conservative person can be just as loving and generous as any liberal. In fact, liberals can be self-righteous and rigid, the opposite of inclusive. The challenge to any person of faith is to remain open to all people and to speak his conscience by example, never by judgment of those who do not see the world as he does.

> *"Politics is the supreme expression of charity."*
>
> —POPE PIUS XI

When Patriarchy Rules

> *"It [God's voice] is the voice of some indistinct Father . . . like Washington's portrait in my third-grade classroom. His face appears wise and kind to those who acquiesce to the assumptions of our cultural canons. But to those who strain and pull against his spiritual grip, the furrows in his brow deepen into a stern warning not to go too far."*
>
> —STEPHEN J. PATTERSON, *THE GOD OF JESUS*

Monotheistic religions are usually patriarchal. A belief in one God was instituted not so much to end the worship of many gods as to bring the worship of the goddess to an end, to eliminate the feminine from the pantheon, and to reserve power to males. The feminine energy cannot be controlled and is subject to ambiguity. These are threatening options to an orderly and well-established male authority.

In addition, a strictly patriarchal religion abolishes our adult power to design a theology or to decide moral questions. The rules that are made by such a controlling institution are not necessarily aligned to advances in psychology, science, and medicine. Thus patriarchal control can mean:

Personal experience cannot be trusted.

Only those duly authorized can be trusted to hold and preach the truth, not necessarily those with mature intuition or sensitive conscience.

The feminine is distrusted and no females are in power.

The granting of grace is limited to rituals requiring authorized/male dispensers.

Revelation is from above, and cannot be added to once the authorities have decided on what is to be included in the canon.

The authorities have the right and power to include or exclude, to decide who is in and who is out, who is a true believer and who is not. *A facilitating religion communicates; a dominating religion excommunicates.*

Order is maintained by threat, by coercion, and by punishment and reward.

Input from the laity/ordinary people is not required in making major church decisions.

A good-old-boy, cronyism network of loyalty allows for cover-ups and mutual protection.

A double standard for males and females obtains especially regarding decisions about one's body.

Heterosexual marriage for procreation is the only legitimate avenue to sexual experience.

Power is legitimized by reason of succession from original authorities who have passed on the keys of the kingdom.

The patriarchal God is on a throne in heaven at a far remove from us, like the authorities.

There is a suspicion of nature, of mysticism, and of the immanent God, none of which can be controlled.

The preservation of the institution and the authority of its hierarchy is the ultimate and unalterable goal of religion.

Religion works hand-in-glove with state authority and makes unquestioning patriotism a virtue.

Authorities pay no attention to low- or mid-level workers nor do they express appreciation but focus fiercely on them if they create notoriety.

Authorities are above the law: the arrogance of power.

All the above principles purport to protect us and society.

In Greek mythology we see the grandfather god, Saturn, devouring his children. This reflects an enduring archetype of the human psyche. It is a metaphor for the appetite of the patriarchy to eat up new ideas, to nip free thought in the bud. Some of these dynamics are necessary in a complex society. "Dynamics" is a psychological term referring to inchoate forces within us—some conscious, some unconscious—that struggle continually. From this battle within us, thoughts and feelings arise that have order and clarity. This is what is meant to happen in human conflicts. The struggle between the young Turks and the old guard is precisely how an integrated synthesis can emerge, how a middle path can be found. The adult challenge, in both religion and politics, is to fight for progress when we are young and not become its enemy when we are old.

An adult certainly honors the role and gifts of certain members of the community and sees them as called to a mission of service. But an adult does not believe that a patriarchal structure is necessary if any contact with God or access to grace is to happen. An adult in faith will not accept theocracy any more than autocracy.

Proprietary theology refers to religious teachings that are meant to validate the claims to power by a specific hierarchy or church. This means that some of what a church proclaims to be revelation from God may be a way of endorsing and perpetuating a patriarchal power structure. We see the necessity for adults to be suspicious of given reasons and look carefully at the history of traditions and beliefs to see what is really going on.

A symbol of maintaining patriarchy in Christianity is in the architecture of cathedrals and churches. The stained-glass windows are meant to teach us by the images depicted on them. They also prevent, however, our seeing out into nature—and the windows are above eye level in any case. Processions were a major ritual in medieval times, so cathedrals have long aisles. The reason given is that the long aisle symbolizes the journey of following Christ on the road of life. At the same time, the long aisle is meant to showcase the full ranks of the clergy during processions. Lay acolytes walk in first and the bishop last with a headdress high and colorful enough to be seen easily. In ornithology the purpose of display, e.g., of bright feathers by a male bird, is to attract toward submission. Political and religious garb can have a similar purpose.

Notice how in both instances, windows and aisles, we are taught a meaning that is theologically appealing while there is another motive, one that is meant to uphold the hierarchical claims of the patriarchy. Our healthy suspicion helps us understand both sides. This double meaning is not new. Psychologist B. F. Skinner, in *Beyond Freedom and Dignity*, related an ancient example of how religion can be used to serve a hierarchy: The pharaohs were "convinced of the necessity of an inviolable tomb by priests, who argued to this effect because of the sacerdotal privileges and powers which then came to them."

The patriarchal nature of a church is not a conspiracy of that religious tradition against our freedom. The hierarchy did not deliberately intend to fool or control us. Control by fear is simply the default setting of any institution with power. We are all heirs of patriarchal systems in religious, academic, political, and military life. Any hierarchy treats us as they were treated, as our parents treated us children before there were self-help books that offered more enlightened ways to bring us up. Now there are many resources, in all areas, with new and more humanistic approaches to religion, accessible to us all. We can all move from default to conscious choice. Adults with faith make that move.

A facilitating religion can open us and provide a vast arena for our free minds so that we can speak prophetically to the world. We do not have to give up our faith because of how it was in the past but rather we have to accept the challenge to make it work in the present. This means cherishing what is good and confronting what is still unreformed.

In the ancient Greek city of Dodona the people revered an old oak tree because they noticed that it had oracular qualities. As news of this miraculous tree spread, priests confirmed its powers and proclaimed them to be from Zeus. Soon after, the tree was set apart as "sacred" and became off-limits to ordinary people. They had to make their requests to the oracle through intermediary priests who required offerings. This is a metaphor for how the patriarchy in a dominating religion can appropriate the spiritual realizations of the people. What began in Dodona as an encounter with nature and a folk-faith in the transcendent fell into the hands of an official priesthood. Male functionaries became the necessary mediators who decided how graces were to be dispensed. But for adults, the sacred oak needs no guardian authority to preserve it. The "it" is, after all, the inner life of nature ever open to and reflective of the powers in every human psyche.

It was not a coincidence that Rome made Caesar a god, and then emperors gods, just at the time Christianity arose. The patriarchal religion of Rome was ready for a more enlightened alternative. Christians were willing to die for a faith that offered just such an alternative to Roman imperialist religion, a virtue unknown in the pagan world. But by the fourth century, Christianity was established and in collusion with the political powers, like the pagan religion it succeeded but the style of which it, sadly, never fully dissolved.

There have been disputes within every church all through history. These days something new is happening. We are no longer arguing with those who see things narrowly and who believe there can be only one way. An adult is so focused on her spiritual growth and in making her faith active that she will not put time into trying to get an institution to come along, unless that has proven useful, that is, has yielded results. She will share her spiritual gifts with those who are willing and able to receive them. An adult says: "Progress gives me hope," not "I am still hoping for progress."

A monolithic church will not change easily. Its concern may be more with self-preservation than with reformation. Some people have a special calling to put in the tireless and draining effort it takes to make changes in institutions. Some are called to be critics, standing outside the institution and pointing to its need for reform. Some are called to be prophets and reformers, standing inside and pointing, often while the fires at the stake are being readied for them. Adults with faith find their place and take their stand, buoyed by prophetic voices, such as these:

Religion has served—in a usually very, very small minority—the function of radical transformation and liberation. This function of religion does not fortify the separate self, but utterly shatters it—not consolation but devastation, not entrenchment but emptiness, not complacency but explosion, not comfort but revolution—in short, not a conventional bolstering of consciousness but a radical transmutation and transformation at the deepest seat of consciousness itself. . . . Transformative spirituality, authentic spirituality, is therefore revolutionary. It does not legitimate the world; it breaks the world; it does not console the world, it shatters it. And it does not render the self content, it renders it undone.

—KEN WILBER

Jesus' prophetic ministry of word and work was not merely a threat to the particular domination systems of Rome and Jerusalem. It was a fundamental subversion of domination itself as the demonic structure operative in human history. The incarnation was God's revelation in Jesus that God is not a supreme power controlling humanity through fear of damnation or extinction, nor the legitimator of human domination systems, but One who has chosen loving solidarity unto death with us to free us from all fear and bring us into the "liberty of the children of God." Jesus was the end of all domination systems, all systems of salvation by the power exercised by a few over the many. No such system, political or religious, could ever again claim divine sanction.

—SISTER SANDRA SCHNEIDERS, IHM,
RELIGIOUS LIFE AS PROPHETIC LIFE FORM

Chapter Three

What About Spirituality?

"The beginning of the spiritual journey is the
realization, not just the information but a
real interior conviction, that there is a higher
power or God or, to make it as easy as possible
for everybody, that there is an Other (with
capital 'O'). Second step, to try to become the
Other (still with capital 'O'), and finally the
realization that there is no other, you and
the other are one, always have been, always
will be, you just think that you aren't."

—THOMAS KEATING, OSB

Spirituality includes the same four elements that comprise religion: beliefs, moral consciousness, ritual, and devotion. The difference between religious and spiritual people is one of style. From the perspective of most institutional religions, we might hear: "I believe in God as I *learned* of God from my religion." Spiritually oriented people add: ". . . and/or as I *experience* God." Thus religion may be uniform in the four elements while spirituality is experiential and unique to each individual. The positive committed response to religion or spirituality is faith.

Religion involves communal experience, reflecting the archetype of community. Spirituality is designed by the individual, reflecting the heroic journey archetype. Religion is organized, with clerical mediation necessary and with an accent on orthodoxy. Spirituality tends to be unorganized, with no special mediation necessary and with an accent on choice. Spiritually we pick and choose; religiously we align.

An unhealthy institutional religion is self-maintaining, forgetful of its universal calling, and hierarchically controlling. This style comes from and instills fear. When we are spiritually aware adults such religion garners our compassion but not our participation.

When we are spiritually aware, we are open to religion when it provides a community that fosters social consciousness and encourages personal growth in love and wisdom. A healthy institutional religion has a collective advantage. It creates a community that works together for social change.

A healthy institutional religion preserves and promotes teachings for later generations. It cherishes a treasury of ancient wisdom and mystical consciousness that is rich and continually appealing. Individual spirituality cannot achieve this but can access it.

A healthy institutional religion includes a prophetic dimension. It's the voice that speaks up to the political status quo or to policies that do not seem morally valid. Spirituality that is personal does not offer this dimension.

We can be religious and not spiritual or spiritual and not religious or both at once. Huston Smith says that religions are to spirituality as universities are to education. You can get there without it but you will be traveling uphill. A facilitating religion provides a framework in which to understand the world and ourselves. Then it can show us a path to love of the world and ourselves. This becomes practice of our spirituality. The difference between a religion with or without a personal spirituality is like the difference between stretching and yoga. The spiritual dimension upgrades a bodily function into a richly expanding experience.

The four elements of religion display themselves in some common themes among people today who say they are "spiritual but not religious":

They *believe* in something that cannot be proven, such as that we all have enlightened wisdom and basic goodness within us and that there is always more than we can see or know, hence there is something or someone transcendent.

They act with a *moral* sense and show it in commitments such as speaking up about oppression, spreading ecological consciousness, and showing loving-kindness toward others.

They engage in *rituals* such as the use of candles, incense, altars, chanting, and affirmations.

They have a sense of *devotion/relationship* to a spiritual or religious figure such as Christ or Buddha or to nature/the universe or to a group such as happens in a Twelve-Step program.

Spiritually oriented people often practice Eastern techniques such as yoga. The same four components also mirror the four yogas/practices in Hinduism as outlined in the *Bhagavad Gita*:

Jnana yoga: knowledge of the self and disidentification with the ego/body in its inclinations toward fear and craving.

Karma yoga: selfless action to identify with all humanity and free ourselves from the consequences of failings from this life or past lives.

Raja yoga: meditation as a ritual discipline of the distracted mind to focus on and enter the eternal Self.

Bhakti yoga: devotion that identifies with God in love and relies on God alone rather than the gratifications of ego with all its props and glamors.

Thus the differences between "religion" as most people understand it and "spirituality" as people experience it are ones of emphasis only:

A dominating institutional religion usually places more emphasis on:	Spirituality usually places more emphasis on:
Membership	Experience
Obedience	Surrender to the givens of life
Revelation from specific scriptures, official declarations, and accepted traditions	Revelation from an inner voice, from nature, and from an unlimited variety of sources
The belief that one religion has all we need	Openness to all religious traditions
One program/practice that has to fit for all	The value of personal practices and a personal journey
Grace from specific sacraments and rituals	Grace is everywhere and available to all with or without rituals
Standard prayers/rituals	Personal communication with the divine and the designing of our own rituals
The use of natural things in rituals	Nature as full of the divine
Requirements of us	Opportunities for us
Limits on choices and behavior based on a moral code and laws	What is free-spirited, intuitive, and conscientious as well
Evangelizing to increase church membership	Sharing the good news about the variegated paths
Saving one's soul as well as caring about the world	Involvement in world politics and awareness of our role in cosmic co-creation

A Cosmic Dimension

Spirituality for some people can mean sentiment or the espousal of new-age beliefs that border on superstition. People may call themselves spiritual when they still have a self-serving moral sense, engage in comforting but not consciousness-impelling rituals, and express devotion to religious figures without the element of imitation of their virtues. Such "spirituality" may be based on a superficial knowledge of religious traditions. It may be "me" rather than "we" oriented.

If spirituality is to have meaning, it has to reflect the culture and needs of its time. Today, with global consciousness, we require a spirituality that focuses on co-creating the planet, growing in social consciousness, and being passionately concerned about justice, peace, and love reaching fully into every corner of life. Spirituality is not only personal but cosmic. Thus we know we are growing in spiritual consciousness when:

> Our love reaches beyond those who are near and dear to all humanity, far and wide.

> Our insight is no longer limited to what we have gained from personal experience but includes perennial wisdom.

> We are committed not only to healing ourselves but everyone, especially in the realm of reconciliation and universal rights.

In the *Bhagavad Gita*, Krishna says: "Those who teach this supreme mystery of the Gita to all who love me perform the greatest act of love" (18:68). Spreading what seems to us to be good news is a natural inclination, a sign of love. An adult's concern is not simply with one's own self-realization but with the spiritual evolution of the planet. We become truly moral when we want enlightenment not just for ourselves but for all beings. Adult sharing is not shown by proselytizing but by example. This follows from adult faith being active, not notional. The motive is to share the joy we have found, not to convince others how right our beliefs are.

Egoic Religion and Spiritually Aware Religion

Rather than divide religion from spirituality we can distinguish spiritually oriented religion from egoic religion. The former is what we have been referring to as facilitating and the latter as dominating. Religion can serve the neurotic ego with all its fears and constrictions. It can also serve the higher Self when its emphasis is on individual freedom and universal love.

Religious teachings can be either egoic or spiritual. Traditional religion, for instance, offers a reward in the world beyond for our good deeds. This appeals to the ego. But the spiritually religious motive for good deeds is simply becoming a loving person. Then heaven is welcomed as a opportunity to go on helping humanity but in a new context. In addition, virtue becomes its own reward, and if others do not follow suit, that does not cancel or derail a spiritually motivated commitment. This mature spirituality is not a strategy to get ahead, to influence others, to gain merit, or to be less stressed. It is about being on earth what one believes that God is in heaven, a supportive love of all that is.

Here is a way of distinguishing the religion of ego from the religion of spiritual awareness. The chart on the following page helps us summarize some of what we have discussed so far:

Egoic religion proposes:	Spiritually aware religion affirms:
Ours is the only true religion, the one true church	We appreciate the wisdom in all religious traditions while we practice our own
Loyalty is crucial and required	We are loyal but with a commitment based on reason and investigation
Our church needs no improvement	We are always in need of reform
We are never good enough as individuals	Our openness to transformation and to new ways to evolve makes us good enough
The afterlife brings eternal reward and punishment	We are concerned with how life evolves and is completed/ fulfilled more than about what may happen after death
Our goal is to keep the institution alive	Our goal is to keep the message alive
Our conscience is formed by obedience to authority	Our conscience is activated by compassion, especially within a group of fellow believers com-mited to social action
We have the right to judge others	We do not judge others but only assess concerns and then become available to those who may need us
We follow strict rules	We cherish values and act on our principles
Our decision-making is hierarchical	Our decision-making is egalitarian
We can judge or exclude others	We seek common ground in ever more inclusive ways
We always know who is in and who is out	We are ever more inclusive in our sense of community
We seek peace and simulta-neously believe that war and retaliation can be justified	We seek peace and reconcili-ation by nonviolent means
We support the purposes of the state	We question authority and support only policies that we believe can promote peace and justice
All revelation has already happened	Revelation is still happening

How Spirituality Makes Love Universal

> *"Here we have a prospect of one common interest*
> *from which our own is inseparable, so that*
> *to turn all that we possess into the channel of*
> *universal love becomes the business of our lives."*
>
> —JOHN WOOLMAN, *QUAKER DIARY*

The face—F.A.C.E.—we are so often trying to save is ego: fear, attachment, control, and entitlement. We have distinguished an egoic dominating religion from a spiritual facilitating religion in which the goal is not fear but love, not attachment but openness, not control but freedom, not entitlement but standing up for justice but without retaliation. The ego would love a face-lift in just those ways. After all, our ego was never meant for extinction but for evolution. Spirituality is how that can happen.

Our work as spiritually aware adults is to free our ego from its terrified clinging to self-centeredness in favor of generous service to the evolution of humanity. We may restrict our affections to a few persons nearest to us. In a world in which survival depends on global cooperation, our life goals can no longer be only about our own immediate relationships. They widen into the practice of universal love. We hear from Albert Einstein: "Now our task must be to free ourselves from this prison by widening our circle of compassion to embrace all living creatures and the whole of nature in its beauty."

This is the point at which spirituality becomes a useful and necessary tool toward a goal that psychology may overlook. Karmayoga is the Hindu way of describing the discipline of selfless action. To have universal love *is* to love God. This, as we saw above, is *Bhakti*, devotion to the divine, one of the four elements of religion and spirituality.

Erich Fromm, in *The Art of Loving*, says that love of God is: "to long for the attainment of the full capacity to love, for the realization of that which God stands for in oneself." This is because our life purpose is to actualize our human powers and unconditional loving is our best power.

As an ego becomes healthier it becomes softer, more pliant. Then love automatically comes through in a universal and unconditional way. As people become healthier, a psychological enterprise and a spiritual trust, they show more integrity and act with more love. For instance, grief for loss is psychological work. Yet it becomes deeper and richer when it includes a spiritual practice that helps us see how a hole in our life can become an opening for the transcendent. Our personal grief then also helps us grow in compassion for others who feel losses as we do. In this way, our psychological work blends with growth in spiritual consciousness. In that sense, it is all psycho-spiritual work and psycho-spiritual grace. This union is the true integration of the psychological and the spiritual, no dualism remaining anywhere.

Our emotions can mirror those of others because our brains contain "mirror neurons." They make it possible to imitate, resonate with, or read others' emotional states and to notice whether their intentions seem useful or dangerous to us. This is how we know whether it is safe to approach or avoid someone, a survival technique. Mirror neurons seem to be dysfunctional in autistic children, perhaps explaining their lack of empathy or connection and their sense of isolation with consequent hypersensitivity. Mirror neurons are found throughout the brain and aid in how we may appropriately join action to perception. They explain how we can see sadness in someone and automatically feel sad too. We are able to be empathic because we can appreciate what the other feels by what we feel. Thus we are *neurologically built* to feel compassion and to experience connection with one another; limitless numbers of others. Even without the advice of spiritual masters we would have been kind—an indicator of how truly innate our goodness is.

Some of the innate urges in the limbic system within our mammalian brain can become moral behavior. Thus in normal development, we are naturally inclined to be morally conscious in such ways as these: to provide for those we love, to protect the weak, to help those in need, to take action to prevent the innocent or the young from becoming victims of abuse. Choices that reverse these natural instincts are how we define evil.

What we might call the limbic virtues are based on the survival of our own clan. Spiritual teachers offer an alternative: to apply our virtues of caring to *all* humans. In this universally oriented spiritual view, evil is more likely to happen when the sense of a common human connection is absent. When connection and loyalty are limited to a family or nation or when we hate those who are different from or disturbing to us, the whole world is in danger.

A world without morality would make for a profit motive of greed instead of equitableness. This is why the civic virtues of the citizens of the Roman republic were reduced to greed and power in the days of the empire. Are we in the same danger in our society? Can religion and spirituality save us by reorienting us? The answer is yes if they are all about love rather than fear, all about proclaiming a lifestyle that interrupts the political lockstep march toward greed, hate, and ignorance. Then spiritual consciousness heals and helps the world by offering the More that it was always meant to be about: justice, peace, and love. Adult spiritual faith is commitment to that More than the world is now.

Showing the Wholeness That We Are

Making our ego healthier happens by psychological work. Growing in spiritual consciousness happens by spiritual practices. There follows a chart that can help us see how the psychological connects to the spiritual. The columns are not separate but rather simply distinguished from one another.

Our psychological work	Our spiritual practice
Growing in self-esteem	Acting with integrity and virtue (habits of wholesomeness)
Self-nurturing behavior with the ability to self-soothe when in distress	Practicing loving-kindess to ourselves and others equally
Healing/grieving our childhood losses, abuses, or diappointments	Forgiving our parents and moving forward in life with compassion for ourselves and them
Building a healthy ego	Letting go of ego fear and craving
Acting assertively in personal relationships	Standing up for the truth in the world at large
Working conflicts out with people and caring about their pain	Committing ourselves to principles of nonviolence and compassion everywhere
Seeking retributive justice: includes punishment	Seeking restorative justice: aims at merciful reconciliation
Being willing to admit our faults and make amends	Forgiving/letting go of blaming others whether or not they are repentant
Reading our experiences and reactions to see where our work is	Noticing pointers to our work in synchronicity and deams
Working on our intimate relationship and on our fears of intimacy	Opening to our partner without ego mindsets and with unreserved loving-kindness
Trusting that the right person for us is not the one who seems to have nothing to work on but the one who is glad to know his work and willing to engage in it	Wanting to join our partner in the lifelong mutual enterprise of exploring inner wholeness
Showing concern for others rather than being self-centered	Practice loving-kindness and attending to the needs of others in acts of mercy
Socializing our behavior so that we can relate effectively to others	Acknowledging our selfish, unkind, or retaliatory behavior and altering it for the better
Taking pride in our accomplishments without arrogance or competitiveness	Believing that grace is at work in us and being thankful
Expanding our personal skills to live more enjoyably and securely	Responding to a personal call to contribute to the welfare of all humanity
Showing love to our own circle of family, friends, and partner	Showing unconditional love to everyone
Achieving our goals	Fulfilling our destiny
All these are the results of the work we do on ourselves	*All these are the results of the shifts that can happen to us by grace*

In actuality, *both work together*. Study this chart and ask yourself how each side can apply to your daily life.

A healthy person combines and integrates psychological work with a spiritual practice so that the listings shown in the chart continually blend into one's lifestyle. Here are some ways this can happen for us:

We transcend our ego.

We acknowledge the oneness of all reality.

We are open to increasing our wisdom and compassion.

We enter the serenity and equanimity that happen when we are no longer driven or stopped by fears and fixations.

We can challenge ourselves to awaken in the same four ways:

To say we are one with all that is means there is no separate anything, including the self. Thus we can free ourselves of self-centeredness.

Then the universe is a holding environment, and we are all in it together, so we take care of one another.

Once we are wise enough to see that nothing can happen that is not a part of us already, we have crossed the threshold from fear to freedom.

Serenity and equanimity result.

A spiritual religion provides a motivation for goodness, something the science of psychology cannot do. Such a religion gives a vocabulary and skill-set for the deepest yearnings in the psyche, something philosophy cannot do. As an example, here are two of Buddhist Jizo Bodhisattva's vows, flowing from a spiritual motivation. Psychology helps us become healthier as individuals but does not get us to this heroic level:

"Only after all beings are taken across to enlightenment will I myself realize enlightenment."

"Only after the Hells are empty am I willing to become enlightened."

Did the religion and spirituality of my childhood so inculcate love that I was drawn to make vows like that or was it about how to save myself? How can I make these vows now?

When people turn against us or act unfairly toward us, we are understandably angry. Yet their behavior is also an opportunity to show loving-kindness, a spiritual practice. They can help us learn how to love our opponents, how to do good to those who hate us, how to bless those who curse us, how to pray for those who mistreat and misunderstand us.

Those who hurt us or treat us unfairly show that they need help, especially from us. In spiritual consciousness, we see that the best way to reach them is to open a dialogue rather than to scorn or hate them. At the same time, we can also declare, nonviolently, our legitimate anger. Our motive is not to shame or convince them but to show our authentic feelings and then to offer our magnanimous love. Then their fear may fade and their respect for us may grow. Once our healthy anger has such spiritual purposes as these, our blame and retaliatory desires vanish. Then our protest against what we feel as unfairness has the tone of loving-kindness in it and others can hear us better. What began as disappointment becomes our opportunity for growth.

This includes our practice of an unconditional yes to such givens of life as:

We do not always get our way.

Justice is not always done.

Others may not defend or even acknowledge our liberty.

Fear can sometimes win the day.

When we say yes to these hard facts, we grow in compassion and realism. We are then more likely to find nonviolent ways to continue the fight so that justice can have its say and day. Our healthy response to the givens that head our way is *how* God is within us. Our refusal to be stopped or driven by fear is *how* God is love.

When we work toward common ground rather than ongoing opposition with one another we begin to see all our interactions with others as opportunities for spiritual practice. Everything that happens from people and events can become opportunities for loving-kindness. This is spiritual faith in action, moving us toward awakening.

We are spiritually aware when we act like what we seek. For instance, when any disturbing experience occurs we can auto-correct/link to how someone we admire might have felt it and would be likely to respond. Likewise, when judgment arises in us, we can auto-correct/link to loving-kindness rather than to our default setting of aggression.

How can I experience this event in wide and deep spiritual consciousness rather than in the narrow and shallow confines of my own ego? This is the question we can ask in any predicament. It redirects our focus from our narrow ego to our higher Self.

Chapter 4

What Is Faith?

*"Modern man has lost the protection
of ecclesiastical walls, erected and
reinforced so carefully from Roman days,
and because of this loss has approached
the zone of world-creating fire."*

—PIERRE TEILHARD DE CHARDIN

We have all heard it said that we have to learn by experience. People can tell us something over and over but until we have the experience ourselves, we are not likely to believe it. We can learn something in a class but not truly embrace the truth of it until we have had some experience that validates it. Likewise, we may believe in something but we are not fully on board with it until we put it into action. It is the same with faith. We may believe intellectually but not have a faith-in-action until we have an experience that leads to a commitment to act in accord with belief.

Belief is intellectual assent based on intuition, imagination, or trust in authority. Knowledge is intellectual assent based on investigation and experience. Faith means belief or trust in something that or someone who transcends us. In that sense, it can be both spiritual and religious.

Many of us were taught beliefs, truth claims, to which we were asked to give assent. This assent was notional rather than holistic if we were trusting in the beliefs of others rather than having an experience that led us to our own beliefs.

As we saw above, when faith is about commitment to action, the more mature style, it becomes more than notional. Then a creed is a list of affirmations that we are committed to put into practice. The path of many modern people of faith suggests orthopraxy not orthodoxy, focusing on practices rather than dogmatic beliefs. Along these lines, Anglican theologian Richard Hooker (d. 1600) said that there are two kinds of atheists: those who don't believe there is a God and those who don't live as if there is a God.

Simple faith is assent to, belief in something as real, without evidence. So believing in a God or being sure there is no God both spring equally from faith. Faith means believing in something that contradicts or transcends appearances. This can be true for both a believer and an atheist. The human ego abhors the vacuum created by uncertainty. Both the believer and the atheist have filled in the void with certitude.

Faith shows up differently in each of the four components that we find both in religion and in spirituality. The paragraphs above describe faith as applied to *belief.*

Faith in the context of *morality* means living in accord with values and principles that reflect our commitment to love and fairness. It is more than following commandments for fear of punishment. It is a personal choice to act with integrity no matter how others act toward us.

Faith with respect to *rituals* means that we engage in them to express and enact a spiritual consciousness. Thus we believe that performing a certain ritual places an intention in the universe that may be of help to ourselves and others.

Finally, faith as *devotion* means trust in a transcendent power, usually personal, that accompanies us throughout our life journey. This fits with the word for faith in Latin. *Fides* means trust that then *causes* belief/confidence. *Credo*

(I believe), in ancient Rome, was based on trusting first and then agreeing that something is true. *Credo* also meant "I commit myself to" when it was part of an oath of loyalty to a military or political leader. The object of *credo* was a person, not a set of beliefs.

Faith is likewise a trust in the ubiquity of grace and a sense of divine presence. We may feel the power of grace in our lives in very specific moments and circumstances. We feel the presence of God or a divine light at special times. We have a sense of relationship to a power beyond ourselves. These are experiences of the transcendent upon which mature faith is built. This is how mature faith is belief in our own experience, no matter whether anyone agrees or confirms it.

Faith can coexist with doubt within a tradition to which we generally assent. Skepticism is criticism as we come from outside the tradition. The opposite of faith is not doubt but certainty. When we are sure, we cancel the need for faith. Adult faith is certainty that there is no certainty. Real faith abides with questions and believes them more profound and far-reaching than any answers could achieve. Faith is satisfied with mystery rather than eliminating the need for it by an explanation. Since both religion and spirituality include the sense of mystery, both require faith.

A Buddhist practitioner once said to teacher Suzuki Roshi at the San Francisco Zen Center, "You talked about the first principle again, but I still don't know what it is." He answered: "I don't know *is* the first principle." Such unknowing in the realm of faith is not ignorance or a lack of interest in the truth. We are neither clinging to ignorance nor craving certitude. Not knowing is a path to fidelity to the here and now where we may or may not know, where we may sometimes know and sometimes not know at all. The mystics in many traditions praised letting go of knowing as a direct path to truth, the apophatic path we explored above. St. John of the Cross expressed it this way:

I entered I knew not where,
And there I stood not knowing:
Nothing left to know.

A person of faith believes in divine transcendence. An atheist believes there is no divine transcendence. An agnostic does not believe either way because he says it is impossible to know for sure. All three may have occasional doubts.

Another option is in *mindfulness.* A practitioner of mindfulness is not a believer, a nonbeliever, nor an agnostic. Such a person can easily be one who has *let go of the need to know at all,* and does not seek to know nor believe that knowing matters. She prefers to sit in the pure space in which knowing and unknowing have become equal. She sits in utter openness to the experience of the moment. She is the fair witness who accepts reality without a need to understand its origin or destination. Such a practitioner does not easily embrace second-hand faith, the faith passed on to her from others' experience. Any person of faith can be like this too.

When we begin in mindfulness, being faithful to our experience in the here and now, the question of permanent religious meaning does not become our focus. We experience meaningful moments, feel meaningful emotions, see and touch things that show or take on meaning. The question of whether there is objective ontological meaning becomes irrelevant. We are content with here and now meanings.

"These are all the wrong questions."

—ANSWER FROM THE SPACE [TRANSCENDENT] PEOPLE
TO WOODY ALLEN WHEN HE ASKED THE STANDARD
QUESTIONS ABOUT THE ULTIMATE NATURE OF REALITY
IN THE FILM *STARDUST MEMORIES,* 1980.

Faith and Fact

> *"The divine mysteries so exceed created human
> nature that even when these mysteries are
> presented in revelation and received by faith
> they remain covered with the veil of faith itself
> and shrouded in darkness as long as in this
> mortal life "we journey to the Lord, for we
> walk by faith and not by sight" (2 Cor 5:6)*
>
> —VATICAN I, *DEI FILIUS*

The realm of fact and proof is not the realm of faith. Here is an example of the distinction: "George Washington was the *first* president" is a fact that has been proven by authentic documentation, so it is not subject to argument. To state: "George Washington was a *great* president," however, is an opinion that can be debated but never fully proven. To do so would involve an agreement about what makes for a great president, and that too is a matter of opinion.

That George Washington was a great president can be believed as a conviction, but it is not in the realm of faith because it is an opinion and, in any case, it is not about something or someone transcendent. In addition, George Washington is not an object of faith, because he is remembered, but he is not *experienced*. But that is what happens to people regarding Jesus, Buddha, and others in whom people place their faith. They experience the objects of their faith as alive now. Thus faith easily grows around them but not around George Washington, who is not experienced as alive but only remembered as historical.

Mystery, not fact, is our focus in faith. The word for mystery in Greek means secret or hidden, known only to initiates. Mysteries were ancient religious rituals that required a laborious initiation by the participants, who then received a living realization of something More than they ever thought possible, e.g., eternal life.

Aristotle noted that during the high point of the ancient Greek death-resurrection mystery ritual of Eleusis, the initiates were not meant to learn, only to experience, and that is true union with the divine. As we saw in the section above, to let go of the need to know, understand, or define shows us what our intuitive and enlightened Self actually looks like. It is silent, still, open—mystical words for the mystery of the divine itself. Editor and author P. L. Travers wrote: "It is from Unknowing that all the myths, and, one may say, all religions issue forth and reveal themselves. Not invented, but, as it were, summoned." Then our faith is in the truth of our personal experience.

In medieval times, knowledge was thought to be trustworthy only if it came from or was approved by religious authority. After the Enlightenment, knowledge was reliable only if it came from empirical science. Both insisted on the "only" path to truth. Today, this is a red flag to those who know that life is More than any "only" can contain.

Now we realize that science speaks to the empirical issues but cannot speak to the value-laden concerns of humanity as religion can. Religion is wise in the world of values but not authoritative in the world of science. We need science to tell us how the leg walks but we need religion to tell us how to make the journey of a lifetime. That is the More than walking.

For example, a physician is needed in a hospital but also a chaplain. The physician offers the healing that centuries of science have found. The chaplain offers the healing that centuries of wisdom have preserved. A satisfying hospital experience will include both.

Religious truth is not a reality alongside scientific reality. In a healthy, liberated, and courageous faith, scientific information continually updates the way beliefs are held. This follows from a recognition that truth is one. Science and religion acknowledge one another's value and wisdom. "Everything true, by whomever it is said, is from the Holy Spirit" was a favorite statement of St. Thomas Aquinas.

An adult in faith appreciates the facts of science and aligns her religious beliefs accordingly. For instance, science tells us that the dinosaurs were not here on earth at the same time that humans were. Many fundamentalists deny that fact, no matter how much data is presented to them to prove otherwise. An adult accepts scientific data and looks for ways to integrate it into her understanding of the Bible—an understanding that scientific study of the Bible has helped us find.

Many arguments about religion fail to make the distinction between belief based on faith and fact based on provable data. Did Jesus' body come back to life? This is a scientific question so it does not work as a faith question. In real faith, questions like that are not useful or interesting. St. Paul says in 2 Corinthians: "From now on we regard no one from a worldly point of view. Though we once regarded Christ in this way, we do so no longer" (5:16). The faith question in the Resurrection is not about the fact of an empty tomb or of a glorified or reanimated body but about a mystery beyond explanations or evidence. Adults who believe in the Resurrection of Jesus are those who have had an experience of Christ alive today and they now work to establish the kingdom of justice, love, and peace that he promised. The miracle is not that God proved Jesus was right but that people found a special way to be good because of what happened to him. That is the equivalent of saying that Easter did not simply happen but is always happening and that is the miracle for people of faith.

Room for Both Science and Faith

Scientific materialism, a form of fundamentalism, excludes the possibility of a transcendent order. It has thereby *disenchanted* the cosmos, to use sociologist Max Weber's word. When science desaturates our experience, we lose access to its further spiritual reaches. Meaning and purpose are then only figments of the human mind, projections that do not exist in the universe itself. This negation, a priori, cancels any possibility of appreciating any larger spectrum in the world than what the human eye can see. Our assumptions then dictate how we see and how much we see.

Religion and Romanticism preserved the enchanted world of meaning and purpose, but we usually thought of that world as a separate realm not validated in the "real" world. Teilhard de Chardin and the conscious evolutionary movement helped us see the luminous unified alternative.

The scientific materialist view is that the world has happened as a result of random forces that were and remain meaning-neutral. The religious and spiritual view is that the world is objectively meaningful. Many people choose one or the other view but there can be a third option. We can commit ourselves to confront and hold the tension of opposites—enchanted and flat—not choose one only.

We do this psychologically when we fall in love. Romance makes the world seem enchanted, meaningful, while the stale workaday world goes on. Most of us easily can accept the reality of the transcendent when we feel it personally, as in romance. Unless we have a similar experience of the infinite in the realm of religion, we do not believe the cosmos is enchanted and meaningful too. Our ego, doubting the transcendent in the ordinary, demands proof of the combination of opposites. Proof is the apposite of fact but the opposite of faith.

Religion is often suspicious of science as somehow disrespectful of spiritual values. "Religion will not regain its old power until it faces change in the same spirit as does science," wrote Alfred North Whitehead. A religion afraid of change will not fit the growing needs of a changing humanity. This is ultimately denying the resources of religion to the world.

An adult-oriented church loves change because it is a sign that a Spirit, a mighty unpredictable wind and uncontrollable tongues of fire, is at work. Such a church is not afraid of the new directions into which it might be led. It loves to go to new places. It is committed to the spirit of evolution and honors the advances of science.

Physics tells us that at a subatomic level, there is no mass, only relationship, no stable things, only an ongoing flow. In physics light is considered both particle and wave. The same is true of our psychological makeup and our spiritual identity. A spiritual consciousness tells us we are not separate beings but rather are connected in mysterious, often elusive ways.

Our healthy psychological life is meant to flow with the givens of life and with a harmony in our relationships to others and to the world. Dualism is contrary to wisdom because it fails to see the unity and becomes entangled in attraction and aversion. This is why spiritual teachers advise against a life that teeters between the attraction that makes us cling and the aversion that makes us flee. When we abide in equanimity, we are being true to who we are and what the world is. All the particulars of my life are meant to come into harmony, that is, into relationship to one another.

Here is an entertaining example of the difference between a fact and the various kinds of truth. We complete this phrase in different ways: "The sun . . ." If we add: "shines," we are factual. If we add: "is a ray-gun," we are humorous and metaphorical. If we add: "whose rays are all ablaze in ever-living glory," we are poetic, quoting *The Mikado* by Gilbert and Sullivan. If we add: "is created by God," we are religiously literal. If we add: "is one of the faces of the divine," we are religiously metaphorical. If we add: "is one with all that is," we are mystical. Imagine how many more directions we can choose!

Firsthand Faith

In most religions the teachings are based on the originator's transcendent or mystical experience, which is then transmitted to us. Religious belief is then not based on our personal experience but comes to us secondhand. We have *inherited* beliefs but may not have *experienced* our belief.

We can distinguish knowledge from experience by looking at an example from our psychological life. We may have noticed over the years that our parents and family members did or do not really see us, that is, they have not looked into us with the five A's, attention, acceptance, appreciation, affection, and allowing. That realization of ours is knowledge. Then one night, after the family has all been together in the old familiar way, we are in our room and we have a *felt sense* of our aloneness, a keen, recognizable sensation of being an outsider. We realize that this feeling is the direct result of, once again, not being seen with the five A's. Now we really know the extent of our exclusion because we have allowed ourselves to enter the knowledge with feeling. That is our *experience*.

Applying this model to a faith example we can consider that we were taught that God is always with us. We thereby had faith that God is present in our life, what we have called a secondhand faith. But in some crisis we suddenly *feel accompanied*. Now we have firsthand faith. The experiential faith is the equivalent of deeper knowledge, true understanding, full awareness. It is faith-in-experience, not simply experience because it refers to that which is transcendent of explanation, unlike in the family example. Notice that in this instance our faith is in the legitimacy of our experience. Our beliefs can be subject to doubt; our experience is not doubted.

To return to our example above, there is comfort in the feeling that we belong to something and are part of a community that grants us a sense of being protected. A family that says it offers that will not be believed unless we *feel* it happening. Likewise, adults will be on hold about teachings and promises revealed in religion unless they really feel them in their own experience.

When faith remains secondhand—does not become experiential— here is what then may happen to the four components of religion:

Beliefs can become dogmatism.

Morality can become moralism.

Ritual can become rote and empty formalism.

Devotion can become superstition.

The challenge for adults with faith is to rekindle the original experience of a religion's founder or to have a personal experience of the divine. Then the four components describe a faith that is spiritually aware and alive:

Beliefs help us structure our lives in accord with a realization in us that a divine plan is afoot in the universe.

A *moral* code becomes helpful in forming our personal conscience so that we become more loving and act with more and more integrity.

Religious *rituals* nurture us and give us a sense of access to the divine and its graces in our daily life.

Our *devotion* warms into a personal relationship to God so that a sense of divine presence happens everywhere and anytime, especially in nature, where the evolutionary plan is most evident.

This is how inherited belief becomes the awakened awareness of adult faith.

Poems, Not Headlines

> *"Logic and sermons never convince,*
> *The damp of the night drives deeper into my soul."*
>
> —WALT WHITMAN

Faith language can be understood more easily if we look at its similarity to poetry. Unlike ordinary prose, poetry does not report facts in a literal or scientific way. Poetry presents words with obvious denotations, but it puts the emphasis on connotations, that is, the elusive overtones and associations.

The connotations of words have been gathered for us over the years by the human collective.

The themes in poetry stretch our imagination so that we can appreciate More about who we are as humans. In that sense, poetry does what religious language does; it shows us who we are at a depth level, offering a welcome descent to a spiritually aware adult. A depth level refers to that which is ordinarily unconscious, unknown to us, but can be suddenly or gradually realized in our experience. Poetry and religious teaching both intend for this to happen.

We know intuitively that reading and writing poetry can contribute something essential to human fulfillment, both personally and collectively. Poetry shows us the More than intellect, the treasury of archetypal themes in our universal unconscious. Poetry evokes them into consciousness. What in religion is called revelation is meant to do the same.

In poetry we feel words more sharply. We let a rich meaning arise in ways that appeal to our senses, thus affirming our full human repertory. In our appreciation of poetry we are gathering and affirming our experiences into a *framework* that has order, meaning, and purpose. A design appears. Indeed, we have an inborn need for a felt sense of design, consistency, and coherence in life with a sense of mystery at the same time. This is what is meant by a dimension of deep meaning, i.e., an *experience* that is communicated by a fact and bigger than the fact. Both poetry and revelation can do that for us.

Poetry is a mystery also in that it cannot really be pinned down to a definition. Like a religious revelation it cannot be fully grasped, only *entered* appreciatively. A poem may open to us as an allegory, a narrative that has a hidden meaning. This is the More, the ulterior and ultimate significance beneath the events described and much grander than they.

Poetry tells of personal experience rather than present-ing information. A datum of information offers a definition but not a felt sense about a certain reality. For instance, we can find the definition of a tree in the dictionary. We can study trees in the encyclopedia. We can know all there is to know about trees and their place in nature. We have found the denotation of a tree, the physics of its growth, the scientific facts about it. But none of that comes any-where near the experience of actually sitting under a tree or in a tree. When that happens, we know tree-ness; we then *relate* to trees. We notice that we and trees were meant to be together. We were born with that sense of connection, but it did not come to life until we climbed or hugged a real tree. Poetry portrays and presents that dimension of our tree experience, its felt connotations. Then we appreciate the larger symbolic meanings too, as we do in a religious revelation.

Poetry also employs paradox, a unity in apparent contra-dictions. In a paradox something seems impossible but it is not impossible at all, a kind of miracle. In fact there is more depth of meaning in a paradox than in a stable, univocal fact. We see how opposites can combine, defying our inclination to single out, analyze, and divide. We have entered the realm of the mystical, where poetry and religious realizations are equally at home.

Both poetry and religion use sound and sense to transmit meaning. Neither uses words decoratively. Both use words and sounds to present complex meanings. Both, like music, use repetition and variation. Poetry and religious revelation speak in evocative language and images. Both engage us in our totality: emotions, mind, spirit, body. Thus they grant an access to wholeness.

Finally, the value of a poem is judged not by its beautiful wording but by how well it fulfills its purpose and whether its purpose is worthwhile. For an adult in faith, this is exactly how the value of religious teaching is assessed. We notice, with joy, that it makes us love more, see with more wisdom, and act as sources of healing in the world around us—worthwhile virtues indeed.

> *"It is not a question of one reality being true,
> the others distortions. One allows us to see
> from here, another from there, a third from still
> another perspective; taken together they give
> us a more complete whole, a greater truth."*
> —MARSHALL MCLUHAN AND EDMUND CARPENTER

When Faith Falls into the Void

> *"There are two absorbing facts: I and the abyss."*
> —RALPH WALDO EMERSON

There are times in life when our faith falls flat and cannot help us at all. We feel no comfort in it and gather no courage from it. We lose our taste for the transcendent. We lose our motivation for spiritual practice. We feel no sense of an accompanying presence.

In such a Void we cannot know what is going on, no matter how smart we are. We cannot second-guess or override this voiding of our power to escape from the Void. We cannot go beyond it even if we try with all our might. There seems to be no More in us, in the world, in God. Then our truly unconditional Yes to our own immediate reality, however unsatisfactory, is all we have to stand on, what feel like feeble feet indeed in such a free-fall abyss.

In this Void of no consolation, no assurance that anything matters at all, our life has become arid. We find no satisfaction in our spiritual practices. Now we notice whether we were using them only as consoling refuges or truly as tools for growth in faith, which sometimes includes a challenging numbness like this. Our prayers seem to go nowhere. The Void purifies our sense of God as rescuer, coddler, comrade. This is letting go of the God designed by our needs in favor of the God that does not yield to design. Now we know if we were seeking the consolations of God or the God of all consolation who sometimes does not console.

The story we tell ourselves is that such a state of mind is all wrong, that this should not happen to people like us, that we must have very little going for us, maybe nothing at all. But when we say Yes to this as a given of life, it becomes a totally legitimate option. It can happen to anyone.

Our challenge is simply to sit in our mood or predicament as witnesses. We become open to seeing what next may happen though not expecting anything in particular. We can allow ourselves to be where we are rather than to jump to an action or a self-criticism based on our story. We can then trust what arises from within as more interesting than what we do to change things externally. This is not about doing now but about being now, the true challenge of mindfulness.

We can use an example of the paradox in the Void: success in managing fear prevents us from ever facing it fully. Surrender to it ventilates our souls so that fear becomes an old pickpocket who has lost his skill to steal from us. How ironic that our ego lives in dread of such a surrender! Avoiding it annuls its arrival today, but it keeps coming back, subpoena in hand. Here we fear what would free us. So we lose when we win. The same applies to the Void. To avoid is to win but lose. Facing our Void is all that will free us from it.

One reason the Void is so hard to take is that we feel the loss of the sweetness of former and familiar consolations. That sense of loss now hits us hard and this time grief does not necessarily end it for us. We can grieve but without presuming it will do the trick of springing us from the Void. Our control is gone. That is terrorizing when our sense of self has become, over the years, identical to being in control. Now all bets are off and emptiness has replaced self-definition.

I went through this experience awhile back and wrote about it in this way: The Void is the terrifying sense of irremediable desolation that occurs for all of us from time to time in life. Sometimes it is triggered by a crisis or loss. Sometimes it happens for no apparent reason. It can vanish as mysteriously as it arrives. The Void confronts us with a stubborn silence beyond our ability to escape or interrupt it. This dark night of encircling gloom is felt only as emptiness, vacancy, a wilderness with no oasis. No amount of self-esteem can override or evade it. It is a condition beyond conditions.

At the deepest level the Void is a terror, a fear of abandonment by every spiritual support. If prayer works, it is not the Void. If activities work, it is not the Void. If anything works, it is not the Void. The terror in this spiritual panic attack is that nothing works to save us from the vacuum into which we have been thrown. The experience of the Void means no foothold, no handle on things, no end in sight, no light at the end of the tunnel. It is not quite adequately described as aloneness, loneliness, emptiness, forsakenness, abandonment, desperation, isolation, or even despair. It is all of these at once but that once feels like forever.

The Void is the shadow side of the mind. It is the hidden, unreliable side of our ego, no matter how functional it has become. To say that "nothing works" in the Void means that the mind, no matter how intelligent or competent, goes bankrupt when the chips are down. Its half-measures avail nothing in the face of the true terror. The Void is the Sherlock Holmes who exposes the ego as the Great Pretender.

In the Void, we cannot defend ourselves as we always have. What a paralyzing experience for the ego, with all its clever ruses, its trusty bag of tricks, its stratagems to maintain control, its belief it is entitled not to have things like this happen. Now it is ambushed by a seditious and invisible militia.

The ego is confronting its actual condition in the adult world: It has no real ground on which to stand securely and it never has, this king of ashes. Nietzsche expresses it well in *The Gay Science*: "Do we not stray as though through an infinite nothingness?" The ego is, after all, No-Thing. This is, paradoxically, the true cause of psychological panic and of spiritual awakening to egolessness. The panic about the Void dramatizes the inadequacy of ego and the spiritual destiny of ego to go beyond its power games and face its utter brittleness. Such egolessness liberates us into the larger truth about who we are.

From earliest life, the prospect of being dropped may have filled us with terror. This is just such a drop from invisible arms. To go into such a free-fall space feels like annihilation—becoming nothing. In the direct encounter with remedy-less and solution-less aloneness, we realize that every clever charm, every gesture, every promise of ever-ready consolation has collapsed. We are being given a direct, unblurred vision of our ultimate condition with a simultaneous crash of the means we ever employed to avoid it. Our usual style is to find that things work, that the world we built for ourselves houses us well. Now we find that there is another side: darker, more frightening, ruthlessly adamant against seduction or cajoling. It allows no loopholes. It cannot be fooled by our coquettishness or manipulations.

The habits, bulwarks, dramas, relationships, addictions, and people that we gathered around us helped us stave off this ultimate moment of truth. They were the "fill-ins" that joined us in the game of avoidance of the Void, avoidance of the full surrender of ego. But all that is really collapsing here is the illusion of security. Only illusion can collapse. Our shell, our armor is being dismantled. Our true inner Self remains. In the terror of this moment, such a realization may not be a comfort. Our main fear may be not being able to die then and there!

Now what? When we simply pay attention to the Void, the inner stagnation may awaken and begin to live in a new way. To face the naked truth about ourselves nakedly is all we can or need to do. The Void is simply the "space" that is ourselves when the space is just space, unframed and unclothed. Meister Eckhart says: "Everything is meant to be lost that the soul may stand in unhampered nothingness." The Void is actually a special grace that takes us beyond the mind and its tricks. *We can now confront our condition instead of using so many consolations and distractions to protect ourselves from it. What an adult option!*

We experience the Void as especially scary because we have been refusing for so long to face the inadequacy of our every defense. This is how we betrayed the fearlessness that was always living within us. Our armoring, our running, our running for help, every thought, every plan, every hope we ever cherished: all were ways of forestalling our inevitable encounter with this dogged silence. The Void is the emptiness we always assumed we had to fill but actually only had to face. "Was every choice I made, every activity I chose, a way of eluding this trickster that wanted to force me into the corner I called Me?"

Our so-called unique characteristics are really a set of standard—even fixated—habits and poses that make life more comfortable for us. At base we are open, that is, not yet filled with meanings, concepts, postures, armoring. Void means void of all that. What frightens us is seeing ourselves without our psychological trimmings. All we have been avoiding all along is our own identity. In the Void, the mind was finally forced to gaze into a mirror of itself. It has seen the simulacrum of its empty face, the pure space that is its actual identity: This is what is meant by "The Void is I." Thus the Void is infinite possibility since it is not any one thing we can conceptualize or touch. This is how it can also be what we have called God. The Void means there is no Other. God and I become a harmony of one. It was good news all along but only when the Void dismantled our ego could we hear it. Shakespeare says in *The Merchant of Venice*:

> Such harmony is in immortal souls,
> But whilst this muddy vesture of decay
> Doth grossly close it in, we cannot hear it.

Actually, the experience of the Void is a summons, a call to the adventure of poise beyond pose, of love beyond fear, of faith without evidence, of Self beyond ego. Such a call can be heard only in silence, the interior silence that happens when we dam our streaming thoughts and worries. The Void grants access to a further reach of our own potential, now beckoning to us to actualize it. The sense of inner emptiness is the experience of ourselves as the alchemical vessel of transformation. Thomas Merton said that "a deep existential anxiety crisis precedes the final integration of the Self." "Existential" refers to what happens when an experience is common to all of us and therapy cannot cancel it nor can faith delete it.

The Void is the threshold to rebirth beyond fear. This is because forsakenness is a necessary ingredient of spiritual maturity. Without it, we might never have learned to look within. We would have trusted only external sources, as children trust parents. Without forsakenness, we would have looked only outside for nurturance. We would have remained mired in the neediness of childhood, never freeing up our plenipotentiary powers of spiritual adulthood.

When we shake the pillars that hold up our temple of defenses, we join in the demolition of our frightened childish belief system. In the rubble we see every false premise, every shred and patch that held our life together, every superstition, and every wish for safety from the full brunt of the human story. This is the edifice that collapses, not the fortress of true supports and nurturance but the stockade of imprisoning delusions. We never had anything to lose but our chains.

James Hillman says, "Moments of dissolution are not mere collapses; they release a sense of personal human value from the encrustations of habit." Dissolution is a stage in the alchemical process of releasing the fearless, that is, unconditioned, Self—the authentic identity we have been avoiding all this time. The Void thus prompts a giant leap into finding out who we really are: *We are love in the habit of fear.* Now we see why we believed we had to maintain control: to avoid an encounter with the inner emptiness that fear disguised. To drop control and face our fear is to open the inner spaciousness that love designed. Such opening is a moment of grace since the Void has shown us the folly of relying on ourselves.

To find ourselves still standing after every muniment has fallen means that we are supported by more than what we believed were our only supports. This is the epiphany of grace, the appearance of the divine, the numinous moment when all that can remain is the ruthless faith that goes on believing, not because life has turned out well but because life has renewed itself once again.

Mindful suspense, mindful presence releases our grasp on time, its regretful past and worrisome future. It connects us to the depths of ourselves where past is preparation for a future that has evolutionary promise. This is because we are feeling the contentment of being here now as no one in particular, that is, as no one with a story. Soon we realize that we are always and already More than our ego personality can contain. It is then a short step to acknowledging that everything else is too. Now faith has grown up.

The Void and Depression

At first glance, the Void sounds like depression. Stressful events or losses and lack of relational support often precipitate depression but not so in the Void. Its origins are mysterious and seem to be part of a calling to explore a new and challenging province in our psychic life. Depression is an illness; the Void is a healing episode on our spiritual journey.

What are the differences between being in the Void and being depressed? They are distinguished in these ways:

Depression includes:	In the void we:
Chastising ourselves and feeling worthless, at fault, even liable to punishment: the problem is "here in me"	Have a sense that something is wrong with the practices of religion and spirituality; they no longer work as they should: the problem is "out there"
Grief	Are disappointed
Physical symptoms such as appetite, weight, and sleep disorders	Experience no serious physical issues
A loss of energy in all our daily tasks	Have less energy but the diminution is mainly related to spiritual areas of life
Diminishment of the ability to think and concentrate	Can think and concentrate in daily life but not in moments of spiritual crisis
Suicidal thoughts	Do not contemplate suicide
A sense of being cast adrift	Feel abandoned by God
A belief that our journey has been suspended	Sense that the Void is a necessary part of our journey
Effective help from medication and therapy	Stay with our experience and share with a spiritual director or friend

Walking through the Valley of the Shadow

The Void is ultimately mind. It is not a real entity. It is a mirror of our own nonsolidity. Void means void of boundaries, as is the true Self. When we sit it out, the Void surrounds us but does not extinguish us. We simply stay as the evening comes. We sit still and allow every feeling to pass through us and go to ground as lightning does when it flashes through a lightning rod. We feel no ground but let our feelings go to ground.

"Lost to myself, I stayed," says St. John of the Cross. We get through the Void (not around or past it) by sitting through its severest threat of annihilation. The practice of mindfulness places us on the path through the Void. *We simply stay in suspense.* We simply sit as Buddha did under the bo-fig tree. We just hang there, as Jesus did on the cross. We lie there as he lay in the tomb. We lie as Osiris did in his temple at Philae, still giving life though supine. He is shown lying in the stillness of death yet in that position he is the Source of light at the end of death's dark corridor. Such a combination of opposites can happen only in the sanctuary of the Self, the All in all of us: "The genuine word of eternity is spoken only in eternity, where man is a desert and alien both to himself and multiplicity," writes Meister Eckhart.

If nothing works and we still survive, we have learned that there is nothing to fear ever again. "I survived without support means I have no need of my usual supports. I am my own companion sometimes. God as comrade can be I. In certain moments, I am the More." This is access to the immanent God.

We also discover a surprising paradox: our challenge is not to fill ourselves. Being a hollow bamboo does the most to help us grow into spiritual adulthood. We embrace total disillusionment with shelters, harbors, and retreats and are thereby free from despair. Despair means no hope to hold onto. That condition is one of the givens of life. When we throw away the hope of rescue or exemption from the conditions of human existence and notice that we still survive, we are liberated from dependency and from liability to despair. We walk the path between these extremes. Then the silence in heaven becomes what is described in a Hermetic hymn: "The angels sing in silence."

When we stay with life processes like these, a new softness happens in our hearts. As Joseph Campbell says: "The mind creates the abyss; the heart crosses it." We become more accessible to the hardy truth of human existence, more open to the unprotected and unsupported moments in our lives. The Void is, after all, only *unconditional being*. It is our experience of existence without the tassels and booties we put on it so we would never hear its thud. This unconditional being is actually our higher Self. It is what the lightened ship of light looks like once the doing, acting, and defending have been jettisoned.

We try so hard to avoid ever having to face the Void. Yet to contain and relax into our own emptiness makes room for a deeply compassionate love to emerge. Vacancy becomes spaciousness, and we open ourselves to all who suffer as we do. This is how our aloneness plays a key role in the release of our unconditional love. It may seem that the Void and all the givens of existence are negative or even punitive. Actually they are the necessary ingredients of human evolution and of true spiritual maturity.

The last line of a poem by the eighth-century Chinese poet Tu Fu is: "I am lost between sky and earth like a gull." We notice in this line that he does not ask to be saved, to be given information about direction or position. He asks nothing, but only notices where he is, as if any "where I am" must be gift enough, a trust in grace. Likewise Emily Dickinson wrote: "Moving on in the dark, like loaded boats at night, though there is no course, there is boundlessness" as if the boundlessness, also without comforting borders or directions, was a grace. Such willingness to be suspended is the best practice in the Void. Then the only prayer is Yes.

Two things attract the transcendent More to us, one is chaos and the other is a yes to it, a highly advanced spiritual practice. For instance, in the *Bhagavad Gita* Krishna is drawn to the hectic battlefield but there gives his helpful teachings. When Arjuna ceases to argue and question but rather says yes to Krishna, he is enlightened. Later, Krishna sums up how the divine presence resides in every experience: "I am the Self that lives in all that is." This Self is pure, non-conceptual, undefined, unbounded, like nothingness. So the Void has proven to us that *Nothing is enough* (understood both ways).

> *"The deepest you is the nothing inside, the side which you don't know. Don't be afraid of nothing."*
>
> —ALAN WATTS

Chapter 5

Practicing Adult Faith

"Hallow every pleasure."

—T. B. POLLOCK,
"PASTOR PASTORUM" (HYMN)

In this chapter we summarize what we have explored so far and outline specific ways in which faith can grow into healthy adult choices and mature spiritual consciousness. We can be adults psychologically but still have a child's way of understanding religious and spiritual beliefs. This chapter gathers our main topics and shows how they can facilitate an adult faith.

We Accept Life's Givens

We notice givens in each stage of life. We notice that happiness does not last; in fact nothing does. We notice that disappointment is part of life. Givens like those may lead us to hope that there is More, something that transcends the givens of ordinary life. Sometimes we feel how More comes through in dreams, in synchronicity, in intuitions, in deep realizations, and in special moments when it seems that grandeur draws nigh unto our dust, to paraphrase Emerson. The transcendent indeed often meets us at the edges and the thresholds, just the places where the hero in every story discovers the More, sometimes fascinating, sometimes terrifying, sometimes both.

In his poem "The Hound of Heaven," Francis Thompson writes: "I ran my heedless ways." This was not an escape but an ironic path. It led the poet to an awakening to the More. Then he was no longer content with the values and kudos of the world. He saw that the givens of life, such as transience and unpredictability, are not penalties but callings to transcend the world as it is while accepting it as it is. That paradox contains a cache of wisdom. We are ready then to see the transcendent possibilities *within* the givens of life. They reveal themselves to be princes, not frogs, as we say yes to them.

We know we have an adult faith when we give up the demand that God rescue us from the givens of life. Givens like impermanence, the unreliability of plans for the future, the universality of suffering, injustice, and betrayal are ultimately ingredients and prerequisites of our own growth as people of greater character and deeper compassion. Then we are the ones who do our best to be enduringly loyal in our relationships, reliable in keeping our agreements, and we do not become agents of suffering. Instead, we look for ways to love and protect others. We act like what we pray God to be or to make happen.

We Are Open to Many Traditions

> *"There are many kinds of eyes. . . . Therefore*
> *there must be many kinds of 'truths,' and,*
> *consequently, there can be no single truth. . . .*
> *Plurality in interpretation is a sign of*
> *strength because it does not rob the world of*
> *its disquieting and enigmatical nature."*
>
> —FRIEDRICH NIETZSCHE, *NOTEBOOKS*

Religion has become "religions," and they sometimes vie among themselves for preeminence. Yet the mystery of life is so great that no one religious tradition can be expected to have all the answers. Even all the traditions are not enough. As we become more adult in our way of living and perceiving, there is no longer only one correct or true religion for all of us. For an adult, religions are *complementary* to one another. Historian Arnold Toynbee said, "There is no one alive today who knows enough to say with confidence whether one religion has been greater than all the others."

The concept of "only one true church" is like the philosophy of colonialism, which states that only one culture is necessary and has a right to absorb all the others. Now with more toleration of pluralism and more availability of theological discourse on the Internet, we are open to accepting the fact that there is truth in all religions. The idea that the mystery of reality can be contained in any one theology is no longer acceptable. The "More than our own" is essential.

An adult will not take any book or set of sacred scriptures as the final word of what God is like or what humans are called to be. The myths that reflect the archetypal realities in us are as reliable as any scripture in finding out more about who we are. Books by Gandhi or the Dalai Lama are revelations no less important than the Vedas. The need to have all revelation completed in ancient times and all now in one place is the opposite of the evolutionary style that everything emerges in history little by little, including revelation.

One of the worst wounds from a religion is the stunting of our imaginations. This can happen when the focus in on making sure we adhere to orthodox beliefs. That approach inhibits, and even proscribes, our capacity to explore. We might doubt our inner wisdom when an authority has to pass on whether our beliefs are legitimate. This is so ironic since faith is based on imagination not on intellect. We feel a wonderful liberation when we find our own truth, free from the rigid dogmatic orthodoxy in which there can be only one correct configuration of life and its meaning.

There is something in us—our heroic journey archetype—that does not want to settle into any single stall, something with an inclination to keep seeking. Our minds are meant to seek and, when we find, to seek again. We humans are not cut out to shut the door on finding more wonders, especially not the door an authority has forbidden us to open. An adult with self-respect has a full and unabashed sense of discovery, with all her powers not only intact but ever-increasing.

> *"There is no direct, permanent, or public access to the divine. Each destiny has a unique curvature and must find its own spiritual belonging and direction. Individuality is the only gateway to spiritual potential and blessing."*
>
> —JOHN O'DONOHUE

We Appreciate Metaphor

> *"The modern world has called us to a maturity we are not capable of if all we have is blind faith and literalism."*
>
> —THOMAS KEATING, OSB

Jean Piaget, expert on early cognitive development, found that children below the age of seven take everything literally. Their brain cannot accommodate metaphor until they are between seven and eight years old. The full ability to appreciate metaphor does not kick in until age twelve.

On bitterly cold mornings in Connecticut when my mother excitedly announced to us children that Jack Frost had been at the windows, we ran to look and imagined an actual artist was responsible for these splendid crystal drawings. In third grade the teacher explained that Jack Frost was not a person, just an expression. In seventh grade science I understood Jack Frost to be a colorful way of describing how temperature and moisture work on glass. Today I went to Google and found out that "Jack Frost" is from a Norse term "Jokul Frosti" meaning "icicle frost." It is also related to the god Ullr in the ancient German pantheon. Now my understanding has evolved so I can appreciate the metaphor, the personification, and its religious overtones—and I still know there is no Jack Frost. The phases from childhood to adulthood mirror those of the adult journey in religion. First I took it all literally, then I saw the metaphor, and finally I appreciated the archetypal depth dimension.

However, in first communion class when Sister Francis Borgia Murphy told us to watch out for the devil and described his red body and horns, I took her to be telling the literal truth and continued to believe that way until adulthood. What was the difference? Sister's statement came with the authority of the church that has the keys to heaven and hell. In addition, Sister Francis Borgia was an Irish-born Mercy nun, and she fiercely emphasized the importance of defending our faith against the anti-Catholic forces in the world—never mentioning Northern Ireland specifically. To hold our beliefs literally meant to hold them fully and strongly, our way of remaining loyal to our religion. In fact, loyalty was basic to our definition of faith. Only as an adult studying Jung and the archetypal shadow did I see that the devil is a personification of the collective dark side of our humanity. But my loyalty to Catholicism has never wavered. Is this because I continue to respect my religion or because loyalty is so deeply installed in my psyche that it cannot be expunged?

Psychological research shows that mental suffering is connected to taking things literally since it derails the power of imagination to present us with healing alternatives. Taking things literally makes us inflexible, and then we cannot cope with anxiety effectively. It is thus not in the best interests of our health to be literal!

Another example from psychology that helps us understand how to work with religious images and teachings is how we deal with our fantasies, especially the darker ones in which we picture ourselves harming others. We do not dismiss them but neither do we have to act them out literally. We look for what need they represent, for instance, rage and the impulse to right a wrong. A fantasy gives us information about our deeper life experience, especially from our past, which we miss if we take things literally. It is the same with religious stories. They tell us what the deep psyche is about. We look under the doctrines and images for what reflects the human journey and how they can help us take it.

Adults do not take scriptures literally but educate themselves so they can be cognizant of the latest research on the literary genre and historical context in which they were written. Literal interpretation of divine events trivializes them and makes them about magic meant to prove a religion's legitimacy. We then miss the many-splendored mystery. Protestant reformer John Calvin said that God used "baby talk" for us, e.g., the creation story, since we are not ready for the full revelation in all its mystical wonder. We notice that the words "baby talk" also indicate that a literal interpretation of scripture is not an adult style.

A simple way to understand the need for stories and images is to look at how our dreams are designed. In dreams the unconscious can only paint pictures. Dreams are visual experiences so they cannot present abstract ideas. Instead they depict them in images. In a dream we see a ladder when the topic is the challenge to climb beyond our humdrum life. Religion does the same. A religion cannot show us ascension, but only tell us about Mohammed rising from the Temple Mount. It cannot show us liberation from oppression, only the Red Sea parting. It cannot show evil, only Satan. Our adult task is to look for the meaning beyond the personifications and story forms. Religious truths are metaphors that are More than historically true. They are metaphors of our own intrapsychic life and our personal and collective destiny, all mysteries about our wonder-filled life.

Eventually, in history, religions come to realizations like these:

Scripture is literary, not literal, meant to be taken as metaphor, not verbatim.

Heaven and hell are literary devices to describe what can happen here on earth, not up in the sky or down below.

There is God everywhere but not a God as a distinct person.

Nature is an epiphany of the divine.

The supernatural completes the natural rather than being divided from it.

There is no magic in rituals, but they can nonetheless enact new consciousness or animate us spiritually.

A person of faith can be sane and psychologically healthy with a belief in a personal God, a supreme being in the sky realm. But he will not have mature adult faith.

A mature person can *know* God is not a being up there but still *think* of God that way. Such a personification is not contrary to being an adult; it is only a maintaining of a link to the comforting religion of childhood. As long as someone knows this, he is believing as an adult, but one who still enjoys his transitional objects. No shame in that.

To say we know God is to deny transcendence, the More than we can know. Theologian Karl Rahner said: "Whoever does not love the mystery, does not know God but continually looks past God and worships not God but the image of God made to our specifications."

The world thrives not on a set of mental constructs but on the love commitments we live by. Indeed, the word "faith in Pali" is *saddha*: "to place the heart upon." Faith for an adult with spiritual consciousness transcends creedal declarations.

It is a vision, a way of seeing the world and responding to its needs. There is then no blind faith, only visionary faith. Losing one's faith can mean no longer taking the propositions of a creed literally. Reclaiming faith means finding the vision it opens.

> *"Blind faith in implausible things*
> *blocks understanding, preventing*
> *the open experience of reality."*
> —ROBERT THURMAN

We See Prayer Differently

> *"What centering prayer does is lessen the*
> *intensity of emotions that surround situations*
> *in which it is difficult to forgive, so that it*
> *becomes more and more possible to reach*
> *out and be open to every other human being,*
> *without exception, all the time, even to the*
> *point of bearing some of their sufferings."*
> —THOMAS KEATING, OSB

A primal human fear is of surrender to reality, also called the will of God. It is hard to trust what may happen, to trust that our own story is a perfect path to wisdom, strength, and compassion. Such surrender makes an unconditional yes our prayer, and the wisdom, strength, and compassion our thanks.

Here is an example of how prayer is related to surrender to reality. In the first step of the Alcoholics Anonymous program, an alcoholic admits he is powerless over alcohol. Yet it is nonetheless possible to recover from addiction. Thus the power to be sober can come only through a higher power than we can muster. A relationship to this power through prayer and meditation contributes to an ever-evolving recovery. Such prayer does not have to be in words; it is a happening. A person ready to recover has given up hope in effort and ego. Instead, he has surrendered his own will to God as he understands God to be. The personal relationship to a higher power and trust in the program of fellow recoverers is rewarded with restoration to sanity.

Remaining present to and ready for what may be is a form of silent prayer since it involves being open to reality, another name for God. When we sit in mindfulness with an intention to free our minds of ego fixations and distractions, there is a neurological reaction in our brain. The thalamus causes the hippocampus, all part of the limbic system, to slow down neural inflows so that less information can enter and fewer mental associations can occur. This results in what in Buddhism is called "calm abiding." We feel there are no separate objects, no time, no boundary between ourselves and the world. Instead, we are automatically contented with what is as it is. The result is more attentiveness, an attitude of listening. *This depth of presence-as-attentiveness is the prayer we were born with, an innate prayer in all of us.*

The adult practice of prayer is not a dialogue from us down here to God up there. The God of adults is too close to be prayed to as a separate person. Once God is a reality both within us (the immanent God) and a reality we are in (the higher Self), prayer is no longer dualistic. We make contact with the divine in ourselves, in all predicaments, in nature. Such contact is prayer; no words necessary. The events of life become personal revelations and grant us a sense of an accompanying presence too. Religious rituals and prayers can lead to feeling better, be it as reality or placebo.

The renaissance mystic and cardinal Nicholas of Cusa wrote: "God is an intelligible sphere, the center of which is everywhere and the circumference nowhere." The interiority of God ("center everywhere") makes prayer a contact with our innermost self. The infinity of God ("circumference nowhere") makes prayer possible wherever we are. Discernment beyond our ego into our deeper self is prayer. Awe at a sunset and honoring it in silence is prayer.

In times of personal trial, we may find ourselves praying to God as a person when we do not believe God really is a person. Devotion makes it possible to address God as personal even if we do not see God that way. Devotion brings intimacy into religious experience. One lover may say: "I adore you" to another, not because he is an idolater but because in love adoration is the best word to express what we *feel*. And surely lovers have a right to hyperbole. In the Hindu tradition, we hear from the twelfth-century poet Mahadevi: "O Shiva, you envelop the whole cosmos but I, by my devotion, hold you in my heart."

We may pray for things that can help us and our loved ones. Even if we believe that prayer does not work that way, our fervent praying gives us consolation and places an intention for a release of divine compassion toward us and others.

Trust in God for an adult entails a sense of a divine presence. This also happens when we pray since prayer creates a field of presence. It is not that we are talking to someone but that a *sense of someone* happens in that field of relating by our prayerful addressing of God so personally. We notice in the twenty-third psalm that David suddenly uses the personal "Thou" when he is in the dark valley that he does not fear since he has so strong a sense of divine accompaniment. To say "Thou" and to feel a relationship to God becomes the same as feeling a presence.

When a prayer is answered, an adult does not imagine that a rescuer/godfather God made an exception for him. It may be synchronicity that what we prayed for was just what was ready to happen. Synchronicity usually grips us powerfully. Anything that does that is a manifestation of the transcendent. In that sense, nothing with real impact is merely psychological.

How does synchronicity connect to a religious attitude? Here are various ways people might perceive synchronicity. Notice that it matches how people perceive miracles and prayer:

> To those with no sense of transcendencc it is mere coincidence, and we choose to give it meaning by projection.

> To those with a sense of the transcendent, it is not merely subjective but inherently real as a message to us from beyond our ego, and miracles are always possible.

> To those with a spiritual consciousness, synchronicity is an archetype of grace, the free gift dimension in life from a higher power and cannot be conjured by our actions, as is promised in superstition.

This is the best of all possible worlds for the world's evolution though it is not always the best possible world for each of us. We are always on the lookout for how we can improve conditions and simultaneously be unconditional about saying yes to what does not yield to our effort at changing things. For an adult in faith, prayer resides in that space and we can always enter it.

Prayer can mean talking to God as we talk to a therapist or lover. We are not expecting that she will make something happen but only help us hold our concern and allow it to open as it needs to.

> *"God give us grace to accept with serenity*
> *the things that cannot be changed, courage*
> *to change the things that should be changed,*
> *and wisdom to know the difference."*
> —REINHOLD NIEBUHR, 1943

We Are Free from Superstition

Superstition is an irrational belief that particular actions or words will lead to a magical result for good or ill. "Superstition" is a Latin-based word that refers to our ability to "stand over," that is, to be able to stand safely above oncoming peril. "If you spill the salt, you will have bad luck, but if you sprinkle the salt over your left shoulder, it will be averted."

Superstition is a revolt against the given of unpredictability by attempting to control it. For instance, if we break a mirror, we can ready ourselves for seven years of bad luck, guaranteed not to be eight. We hold on to superstition to manipulate mysteriously fateful powers so they will satisfy our ego needs and assuage our ego fears. We may use religion in that way too.

A superstitious ritual may be useful at times. For example, chanting for prosperity leads to more focused awareness and can even result in a sense of the power in us for more altruistic purposes. Likewise, repeating a mantra may be useful as an affirmation.

Simple rituals may become superstitious. For example, we sing the national anthem at a ballgame and feel a sense of patriotic comfort. That is an appropriate ritual. It becomes superstition if we believe that our singing of the anthem will help our side win. Likewise, burning incense cannot ward off evil, but it can help bring our focus to it. That and the fragrance are the comforts in the ritual. To believe that the incense has a magical power in itself makes it superstition.

Many superstitions are medieval and based on a belief in an uncontainable force of evil, a devil who prowled through the world seeking the ruin of souls. Incense is the smell he finds most repulsive, so it was used in religious services. Bells make the sound he most dislikes so they are rung in churches to keep him away. In addition, bells were believed to emit the only sound from earth that could be heard in hell—to torture the damned with a constant reminder of their loss. Hell was considered a place of fire and fire is red, while heaven is blue, what Satan is not allowed to see. Baby boys therefore were covered with a blue blanket since Satan cannot see blue. Girls were blanketed in pink since he wants to avoid seeing more of that color.

We can understand superstition and its relation to belief in the power of chance by comparing haruspication and sortilege. Haruspication refers to the belief, practiced in ancient Rome, that a specially qualified priest could foretell the future by examining the entrails of a sacrificed animal. Sortilege refers to foretelling the future by drawing lots. No special power or office is required; anyone can play. Haruspication is superstition since there is no connection between an animal's entrails and the future, especially since the anatomy of a species is basically the same. But in casting lots, we are learning what course to take from chance, the only alternative if reasoned choice does not suffice. It makes all the players equal regardless of rank, gives them all an equal opportunity, and all agree beforehand to accept their lot. On the rational level, it is certainly a useful way to make a decision though it seems to be simply superstition.

Sortilege of many kinds can also have a quasi-religious tone according to Jung, who says: "There is no room for chance in the meaningful world of the psyche." He basically trusts chance to lead us to truth. So casting lots, playing the Tarot, tossing coins in the I-Ching, and attending to astrology can reveal something to us, even clues to our destiny, since they work by synchronicity, meaningful coincidence. We toss the coins in exactly the pattern that is expected to relate to our present concern. Thus for Jung sortilege is not superstition though it would be superstitious to trust one throw of the dice rather than to check it against other events that confirm it, e.g., other synchronicities, dreams, intuitions, advice from a wise guide. This takes chance out of the realm of the irrational and makes it arational, a realm beyond the rational or irrational—the More than rational.

Ultimately, superstition is a lack of faith/trust since it is a belief that unseen forces are stronger than the power of Spirit. To be religious is to believe that there is a higher power, a reality that is More than ego. Most people of faith believe that this power has a loving intent toward us as well as a zeal to communicate with us about how we can evolve toward our own fulfillment and contribute to the betterment of the world. This higher power/God is often believed to use chance, synchronicity, dreams, visions, intuitions, and almost anything, to contact and guide us toward evolution and fulfillment.

The new-age movement sometimes presents us with the superstitious promise that the mind can become sovereign: "You make your own reality." The belief is that our pure intentions will make life happen in a particular way, enable us to shape the way things will work or work out. Such hyperbole seems to be fueled by a sense of outrage that we should be so ordinary as to be subject to the givens of life that apply to other people. If only we can make our spirits pure enough, our intellects bright enough, the new age seems to say, we shall have all we want. We may think a ritual is working for us in this or in any ego enterprise. Yet since our unconscious can be trained by affirmations or mantras, that may be all that has happened.

The belief that absolutely everything that happens is the result of how we think is, of course, another form of superstition. We caused our own cancer or decided to be poor are ways of affirming that our ego is in full control of all that happens. "We chose our parents" even extends our control to before our birth! Beliefs like these disregard and disavow the presence of unconscious forces, of spiritual powers, of grace.

Superstition is sometimes related to fate. For an adult with faith, there is no such thing as fate. There are happenings that are givens of life, e.g., accidents, illnesses, good or bad predicaments, temporary or final. But there is no fate as fatalism, a predetermining force, an inevitable stage-set of consequences, a story about us prewritten and slated to happen no matter what we do.

The ancient Greeks believed there were three sisters called the Fates, who spun the threads of life, both those of gods and humans. This was a way of saying that fate is greater than any god. To believe in God in an adult way makes fate impossible, unless fate is synonymous with a divine plan. But the divine plan includes human freedom so it is contrary to fatalism in any case.

Belief in miracles is sometimes thought of as superstitious. In religious faith, miracles are not superstitions. They are unusual instances in which natural laws are stretched or suspended as graces to us from a transcendent source. Superstition is an irrational belief in a cause/effect relationship when there is none. In faith in miracles, there is a connection by synchronicity, a meaningful coincidence that seems related to but not caused by prayer.

We might also see the miraculous in certain events that science can explain, as in this intriguing example: The Ganges River is honored by Hindus as having miraculous powers. Indeed, it has purifying powers since scientific studies show that the water does not promote anaerobic bacteria as ordinary water does. Thus its healing powers, honored from ancient times are validated in modern science. This does not cancel the miraculous; it simply locates it in nature where the divine lives so vividly.

If there are miracles, then all religions have them. They are not to be considered possible only in our own religion or as proofs that our religion is the true one. A central teaching of all religions is that grace can come to anyone.

Finally, what we call miracles might be instances in which certain beings already have the powers that we all may someday have. The miraculous events are then predictions about and indications of the rich spectrum of human-divine potential.

We Are Free from Obsession with Religion

It is useful to consider the connection between superstition and the obsessive-compulsive disorder. When there are few healthy adaptive mechanisms in our repertoire of responses to stress, we may turn to rituals and superstitions for a sense of security. Overwhelming and usually baseless fears can drive us to actions we believe have magical qualities. The fearsome thought becomes an obsession, and the action becomes a compulsion. Obsessions usually increase anxiety while compulsions temporarily relieve it. They seem automatically to stave off a dreaded consequence, which is why they are in the same category as superstitions. Compulsive actions, such as constant hand-washing, provide a false sense of security and control over an unruly life in which disease is presumed to be everywhere and unavoidable. This sense of safety is the essence of the neurotic control that underlies superstition.

Obsessive thoughts differ from delusional thoughts. In an obsession one realizes that one's thoughts are not valid, and in delusion there is no such awareness. People who suffer from obsessive-compulsive disorders do not welcome intrusive thoughts; they try to avoid them, though unsuccessfully. Delusional people entertain the thoughts and share them proudly, or even forcibly, with others.

We all experience some unwanted intrusive thoughts. The healthy response is to notice them, label them as inappropriate, not assign any meaning to them, not blame oneself for having them, and focus on something else. This can happen more easily for us if we have practiced mindfulness.

The person who suffers from an obsessive-compulsive disorder, however, interprets the thoughts as warnings of danger that require a ritualized response. People who are likely to have this problem have three characteristics reminiscent of some religious upbringings: They were taught to be excessively responsible and conscientious early in life.

They were inculcated with a rigid sense of duty. They did something that led to harm and were blamed for it or they blamed themselves.

A religion that insists on specific ritual requirements for salvation panders to this disorder. Since a religion also offers comfort and a sense of safety, it is often difficult for some people to let go of archaic behaviors even when, as adults, they know them to be irrational.

People certainly can become obsessed with religion. The word "fanatic" is related to an archaic word *fane*, which means shrine. A fanatic is one who cannot leave the shrine. He has become alienated from mainstream living because of an addictive attachment to religious ritual. The word "addiction" is from the Latin *addicere*, which means "to give over" or "to surrender"—in this case to our compulsion.

How can we notice whether we have a religious obsession, an addictive style in our religious life? We can visit the four elements of religion and spirituality for a possible answer: belief, morality, ritual, and devotion. Here are examples of what they might look like in the context of religious addiction:

We are constantly concerned with what the true *doctrine* might be and how to break the code of its mystery—often trying to convince others to join us in our belief.

We are scrupulous about *morality*, never sure we are really doing what is right, often disregarding what is good for us and others. We are afraid of hell, unable to release ourselves from guilt.

We engage in frequent *rituals*, practiced with meticulous attention to detail, that we believe will keep us safe or save us. People who become severely exact in their performance of rituals may suffer from obsessive-compulsive disorder. They may also be caught in the superstition that precision in every word and rubric is necessary for the ritual to work. This is a loss of trust in how grace comes to those who are sincere without having to be perfect.

Devotion has become an attachment to a God or saint as if he or she were a palpable companion, sometimes one who takes the place of a human partner.

In delusion, we might believe that God is telling us to act in certain ways. We may be drawn to religion as we are at times to a relationship or career. We are attached to the dramatic story we are part of, with pride about the special role it seems to offer us. This may be a form of inner entertainment, an addiction to drama and adrenaline, often just what obsession is about.

Problems of obsession and compulsion do not easily respond to self-help practices. Therapy is required. The religious nature of an obsession may make it seem as if we do not need help from the science of psychology. This further keeps us stuck. There is pain in an obsession as well as in a compulsion. Therapy, both psychological and psychiatric, can be a healing resource.

In Milton's hell we see a humorous example of religious obsession. Some demons are punished by being forced to keep thinking about things that cannot be resolved. They can't stop being inquisitive but they also can't find an answer:

> Others apart sat on a hill retired,
> In thoughts more elevate, and reasoned high
> Of Providence, Foreknowledge, Will, and Fate—
> Fixed fate, free will, foreknowledge absolute—
> And found no end, in wandering mazes lost.

> —JOHN MILTON, *PARADISE LOST*,
> BOOK II, LINES 557–61

Finally, I share this poem that seems to fit the subject in my own experience. A *ghazal* is an Arabic form of a poem requiring at least five couplets with the same meter, the first one rhyming. The last phrase of the first couplet has to be repeated in the final words of each succeeding couplet. One's name has to appear in the last couplet. I used "richly loved" since my last name is Richo. My first name, David, is Hebrew for "loved." Since King David was loved by God though he had many doubts and made many mistakes, this fits the theme of my poem—and of my life:

GHAZAL TO THE HOLY GHOST

Pondering God, no way to be released,
Plaguing me still from decades long deceased.

My head is swayed by thuribles and bells
That chime in me from decades long deceased.

I treasure my beliefs as living truth.
I'm sometimes sure they may be long deceased.

Is this obsession or the way You call,
O Herald for whom nothing is deceased?

Am I insanely stuck or richly loved
By You who woos when decades are deceased?

We Ponder the Afterlife

It is part of adult living to educate oneself about the enduring questions that have plagued humanity. What happens after death is a universal conundrum. Faith always seeks understanding. An adult in faith will look into this issue as a way of becoming as informed as possible. What follows may help us with that project.

"Death is the impossibility of further possibility," according to philosopher Martin Heidegger. In the traditional faith view, death is not an end but rather a threshold to the possibility of full actualization. No one *knows* what happens after death. Faith for a mature adult is about living lovingly now and does not become obsessed with what follows death. But a person of faith does enlighten himself about how the afterlife has been regarded in the course of history. What follows may contribute to our understanding.

Plato taught that the soul is immortal by its very nature and therefore cannot begin or end. From this perspective, there is both an afterlife and a beforelife. In the traditional monotheistic religious view, the individual soul is immortal but not eternal. It is created by God in the womb and has no prior existence. But it lasts as itself forever.

In late Greek antiquity the dead were thought to go to an underworld where they would stand before the throne of Persephone, queen of Hades, for judgment. Some would be given eternal happiness in the Elysian Fields. Others would be punished in Tartarus.

Rituals could influence life after death. People could find help in reaching the eternal reward through the initiation rites at Eleusis. They took place every autumn and they made the participant an adopted child of Demeter. Thus when one faced Demeter's daughter Persephone, she would judge him as a family member, not as a stranger, a distinction of great importance in Greek society. This may help us understand such concepts as "adoption as children of God" in traditional theology. The pagan Greek belief in heaven and hell is perhaps a reflection of a universal archetype of judgment following death. Awaiting a final resurrection is certainly a universal archetypal longing.

Buddha in the *Anguttara Nikaya Sutra* promises that those who practice loving-kindness on earth will find and join a community of fellow practitioners in the Brahma heaven after death. This is remarkably like the Christian view that heaven is a messianic banquet, a continuation of the earthly Eucharist. It also recalls a statement of St. Thomas Aquinas: "Faith is the foretaste of the knowledge that will make us blessed in the life to come."

The earliest clear belief in resurrection hearkens back as early as 1500 B.C .to Zoroaster, a priest of the Persian magi. His religion virtually ended with the advent of Islam, though today there are still about one hundred thousand believers in India and Iraq. Zoroaster preached a sky heaven of reward and a hell punishment under the earth. Resurrection of the body was to happen when the world ended by fire, and then the natural world would become the new heaven. He promised a future messiah, Saishyant, who would overcome evil and raise the dead, elements of the apocalyptic tradition.

The Hebrew Bible makes no mention of a heaven-like afterlife until the last chapter of the book of Daniel, which prophesies a rewarding afterlife to martyrs. This was believed by many Jews in Jesus' time, over 150 years later. Before then salvation was thought to be an event meant to happen here on earth through liberation from oppression, e.g., freedom from Roman rule.

Afterlife for the Pharisees in Jesus' day meant resurrection of the body at the end of time. This apocalyptic view includes a judgment and then an eternal heaven or hell. St. Paul was a Pharisee. For him, since Christ was already raised from the dead, the end for everyone was already happening. Paul shows himself to be an apocalyptic believer in that he taught that transcendent evil forces control some human events as well as our bodies, choices, and motivations. We will explore the apocalyptic view in our last chapter.

Early Christians believed that the soul was not intrinsically immortal but made so only by the resurrection of Christ and by faith in the resurrection. Eschatological fulfillment is then a divine act of grace rather than automatically following from the fact of immortality, as in Plato's view. Instead, it is the result of a special commitment to God.

The fact that actions have consequences most likely led to interpreting a natural event as reward or punishment, not as a given of life: "She became sick because of how bad a person she has been. God punished her." The ego's favorite sport is retaliation, so it thrives on statements like that. The "God" in the statement is playing the role of the human ego. A spiritually rich religion is one that honors the givens of life with its random, chosen, or imposed pain and happiness. When God becomes the deputy of the ego, the one who rewards and punishes in this life and the next, we have an egoic religion, not a spiritual one. When the afterlife is connected to the reward-punishment model, it assures the entitled ego that all will be fair after all.

In human experience, torture is used to induce a confession. But hell is permanent torture as endless punishment. This belief configures God as less advanced in compassion than the worst human. To let go of a belief in God as torturer makes it possible to trust in divine goodness, which never gives up on us.

As an alternative, the third-century theologian Origen presented the optimistic notion of *apocotastasis*, a final fulfillment of creation at the end of time rather than a destruction of it. In this view the salvation of every human being, as well as of Satan and all the demons, without exception, is the final victory of God over evil. This means no eternal punishment but rather a final reconciliation of all beings with one another and with God. This doctrine was condemned by the official church.

We see the same concept that was propounded by Origen in the Qur'an, where Satan is to be forgiven at the end of time. It also appears in chapter 16 of the *Bhagavad Gita*. Krishna speaks of those who act from evil motives but does not consign them to an eternal hell, only birth after birth until they learn to be kind rather than to cause harm. This is something like the Christian doctrine of purgatory, in which souls continue to work on their salvation after death as a final preparation for heaven.

Some concepts of the afterlife include having the dead help those who are still on earth. This fits with the traditional teaching in Buddhism in which an enlightened person, a

Bodhisattva, keeps coming back in birth after birth to help all beings find enlightenment too. Here is a similar example in Christian mysticism from St. Therese of Lisieux: "I will spend my heaven doing good on earth."

Generally, religion offers a conquest of death, an ancient desire among humans throughout history. It is in the nature of consciousness to fear death, but that fear is not present in the unconscious, which seems to know that it cannot die. Indeed, in the Jungian archetypal view, the unconscious sees death not as an ending but as a transformation, as the dreams of so many people nearing death seem to indicate. Ego has always wanted that deathlessness. All that dies is the difference between us and the universe. Ego is integrated into the higher Self, in accord with its original and final destiny, the one we were meant to commence during our lifetime. This integration of ego and Self is why we were given a chance to live.

Afterlife has often meant reconnection with our origins, a return to our past, not only a life in the future. Thus the cross where Jesus died was thought to be located at the very spot where Adam was buried. Calvary was the center of the world, where it was created, and where the door of death opens. This *axis mundi* is the center and boundary of the world, so the center and the circumference of earth are both sacred space and sacred time. The ancient Greeks had the same belief about Delphi, the navel of the earth, the center of the world. Eleusis was the sacred place where the door of death opened into eternity.

Likewise, sacred time refers to a simultaneous moment for creation and the end of time. In this combination of opposites all time and places meet. Niels Bohr, quantum physicist, in his theory of complementarity, states that opposites are two aspects of one reality beyond our limited mind's comprehension. Thus a law of physics turns out to be at one with the religious mystery of oneness. Indeed, Bohr used the yin-yang on his heraldic coat of arms.

For some the joy of a lifetime is lessened when they focus outside it for its meaning. Life is a continuum rather than an antechamber. In that perspective the best attitude is to live our life fully now so that we have no unlived life left over at the end of our stay.

Finally, in Zen Buddhism there is no afterlife. Zen master Shunryu Suzuki, after visiting Yosemite, recognized the waterfalls as a metaphor about our lives: A river flows as a unity, then falls over the cliff and becomes droplets that go down to form another single river. Our collective humanity is the river. Our individual selves are the droplets. The time it takes for the water to fall from the river above to the river below is our lifespan. We are the falls between the two rivers of before and after we were here. We do not disappear but rather become one with all that will be, just as we came from the all that was.

> *"I was waiting for you. I wanted to say good-bye before the divine in me departed to the divine in all."*
>
> —PLOTINUS ON HIS DEATHBED, TO A FRIEND

Chapter Six

What Is Meant by God?

*"What is it that breathes fire into the equations
and makes a universe for them to describe?"*

—STEPHEN HAWKINGS,
A BRIEF HISTORY OF TIME

Out There or In Here?

There are two main historical traditions about how God
might be real: as transcendent and/or as immanent.

The word "transcendence" comes from Latin words
meaning "to climb over or beyond." Thus anything that
exceeds or surpasses ordinary reality is transcendent. Within
the human psyche, the transcendent is the higher Self, a reality beyond the limits of our conscious ego.

In religious teaching, God is transcendent because God
is believed to exist above and beyond the material world.
Knowledge of God in the religious context is then considered
transcendent because the human mind is not equipped to
comprehend who God is. "Once you can say: 'I understand,'
what you understand is not God," St. Augustine says.

For a person of faith, God wants contact with us so God
tells us about who God is and what God's will is: a society of
justice, peace, and love. Since our life purpose by faith is to
fulfill that will, a "Thy will be done" is the same as fulfilling
ourselves and advancing human evolution. Thus revelation

tells us our own and our collective destiny. Revelation can be a communication from a source beyond us, but it is nonetheless an intrapsychic event. Intrapsychic does not mean merely psychological but rather a reality that exists in our very being, not as separate but as our ultimate reality. Intrapsychic means within us but nonetheless transcendent of ego.

The conventional theistic view places its accent on a dualistic transcendence: God is an entity beyond the limits of time and place and beyond human understanding as well. So whatever is true of our world and time must be the opposite of what God is.

One common form of this view is that God is a supreme Being/Person, omnipotent and omniscient, who created all things, and is living in an eternal heaven, which will be the afterlife of those who believe in him and act with moral uprightness. Usually referred to as "He," this God can be supplicated by prayer to intervene in human events and to perform miracles. Indeed, our word "God" is from the German *guth* or *gott* which derives from a Slavonic word meaning "what is invoked."

This God is believed to intervene in some instances and not in others, for some people but not for others, though he is adored as all-good and worthy of everyone's love. German theologian Rudolf Otto described this "wholly other" God as a "mystery both awe/fear-inspiring and fascinating." Humans therefore stand in awe of this transcendent God but are also drawn to him.

God as transcendent of any metaphor, as the Wholly Other, is more mysterious but dualistic. It might be more illuminating to refer to God as the "Wholly Under," a formulation that would be immediately comprehensible to mystics, especially because, even in ordinary experience, we cannot see the depth of the ground that supports us. God then *under-stands*.

Another option is to say that God is not the wholly other but *the wholeness of no-other*. This fits with transcendence not as referring to a God above and beyond us but rather that we, and all that is, live in the divine, a life bigger than ourselves. Then God is not up there and we are not just down here. God is what we mean by the atmosphere, the sphere in which we live. St. Paul, perhaps quoting the Greek philosopher Epimenides, says: "In him we live and move and have our being" (Acts 17:28).

Plato did not believe in the physical reality of the gods, but he did affirm that we are influenced by forces from a dimension of being that we do not understand, More than humans can know. This is a way of believing in the transcendent but not as a person or entity. Plato understood material things to be reflections of primal divine ideas, archetypal exemplars that existed in a realm beyond time and place. His philosophy contributed to the sense of God in Christian theology.

In another theistic view, the accent is on God as *immanent*. God is then configured as a reality dwelling deep within us and throughout the universe. "Deep," like "beyond" and "above" are spatial metaphors, but the reality transcends human language or understanding. What we call the soul may best resemble what is referred to as God within. The immanent God is that which is More than who we are but simultaneously the essence of who we are. Thus the immanent God does not fall prey to the dualism that happens in a purely transcendent view. God is not an entity but a force or energy in our psyche and in our universe as well.

The immanent God is an everywhere abiding transpersonal *presence*. Presence is a more accurate way of describing a far-ranging field—as of gravity—rather than a discrete person. However, since the immanent God is More nonetheless, God is present within us and in the universe *as transcendent*. Thus both traditional views ultimately reckon God to be transcendent and immanent at the same time. Raimundo Panikkar says, "God is the transcendent mystery immanent in us."

The immanent-only God does not intervene in human affairs as a rescuer, a *deus ex machina*. God instead is present in every person, reality, and event and therefore all that we are and all that happens are part of an unfolding divine design.

Panentheism, God is in all things, is most appropriate for a view that sees Spirit in the visible world. Then the universe is itself an epiphany, a revelation of God since it contains an inherently divine reality. In this view, to say that God is a person does not compute since to choose a human genus would logically also necessitate further qualities that characterize all persons: gender, sexual orientation, handedness, psychological type, and so forth. Since any of these implications of personhood would be limiting, the result would not be an infinite God. A personal God would turn out to be more like the Greek gods, who had just such individualizing characteristics.

From the evolutionary perspective, God can be understood as personal in the sense of having conscious awareness, but not anthropomorphic. God has personness but not personality. God is the name for the Thou in all that is. Thus we know God when we know ourselves or anyone as a person, each a unique instance of the vast Thou of all that is.

The immanent God, on the other hand, is not someone else, something else, or somewhere else. Since this God is not a person, there is no gender bias making God masculine. Instead God is the loving intention in the universe, the energy that transforms being into inter-being. This makes the divine a presence awake within us rather than a person out there watching us. Expectations of what God will do for us turn into aligning our personal intentions with God's divine plan of evolution.

The transcendent God speaks from Mount Sinai, and his words are recorded in scripture. The immanent God speaks through intuitions, dreams, visions, and unusual moments of awakening. This God also speaks loudly in synchronicity, meaningful coincidence, which shows how our predicaments point to spiritual possibilities on our unfolding path. We may then feel *addressed* by what happens, as if by a personal voice. That experience is the equivalent of what traditional theists call revelation. However, it is not tied to some long past event, but a Sinai moment in the everyday world of our life and story.

In this integrated view, we can know that God is not a person but we can nonetheless personify God and talk to God in the traditionally theistic/transcendent style. Our form of devotion as knowing, talking to, or loving God as a person becomes a way of feeling intimate—and cared about too. As we saw above, an adult can have devotion like this while not perceiving God as dualistic. For instance, educated Japanese people might know that Amida Buddha is a representation of the absolute, not a personal entity. But the image of the compassionate one is nonetheless important to their spiritual growth and comfort. This appeal to the imagination helps us humans toward a sense of something More in the mortal world, a More that wants to hear and be with us.

Transcendence means *beyond* our comprehension and dissimilar to any other reality known to us, i.e., a mystery without limit, impenetrable by thought or concept, inexpressible and inexhaustible by any image. This is expressed well in the Tao Te Ching: "The Tao that can be named is not the authentic Tao."

This sense of how mystery transcends us is reminiscent of the Heisenberg principle of uncertainty in quantum mechanics. It holds that some pairs of physical properties, such as position and velocity, cannot be fully or precisely known. Heisenberg states that this is based not only on our methods of measuring but on *something in the nature of things* that does not ever yield to full revelation. That something is mystery, an inherent fact about any reality including God.

The immanent *and* transcendent God is an indwelling presence in all things and yet beyond any one thing. The transcendent and immanent God as one reality resolves the problem of exclusive opposites, e.g., subject and object, male and female, spirit and matter, beyond and within.

Persian poet and mystic Rumi was asked why he was dancing when it was time for prayer at the mosque. He replied: "The mosque is in the heart." Rumi also said: "Take away the Kaba in Mecca and all the people are prostrating themselves to one another." This chart summarizes the distinction between the transcendent and immanent traditions:

The transcendent God is:	The immanent God is:
In heaven	In us and in all things
The creator of all that is	A driving force within evolution, endlessly emergent, ceaselessly creating
Wholly Other, perfectly complete	Intimately present, ever-evolving
Meting out rewards in heaven above and punishments in hell below	Revealing a heaven that is already here, as is hell, based on our choices
Making some things holy	The holiness/wholeness of all that is
Trusted to intervene in our affairs sometimes, especially if we ask fervently and often, or if we promise something in return	Trusted to remain present and to guarantee that our capacity to love will endure no matter what happens to us but without a promise to change things for us
Wanting us to pray to him with a guarantee that he will listen	Wanting us to contemplate divinity in all that is, especially in ourselves, that is, to live prayerfully
The totality above limitations	In every local reality as the totality
Thanked as the dispenser of graces in accord with our behavior and his will	Thanked by our surrender to grace-filled events

In both traditions, what is thought of as the God/Source is considered unconditional, that is, beyond conditions or stable attributes. Pagan mystic Plotinus made this point when he distinguished the God who is the Self from the ground of being, which he called "the One [oneness] without characteristics." He also used a spatial simile to express his mystical experience of fusion with the One: "the flight of the alone to the Alone." Plotinus added that mystical union was like having light so flood our vision that all things become illuminated but all we really see is the light that is illuminating them. According to Plotinus, in all our inner life and in all the universe we see only the Godhead, the light on, in, and behind impermanent appearances. Life exists within, between, and around us, and the core of that life is called God. This is how we can believe that God is everywhere and everywhen and everyone rather than somewhere or someone living far off in a region of no when. The human and the divine are related as the surface and the depth of a single reality. Thus a more precise word for immanent is *intimate.*

> *"God is our experience of the energy that makes us whole. The human being cannot get enough of such energy and the life it funds, nor can God get enough realization in human life thus funded."*
>
> —JOHN DOURLEY, OMI

The Supernatural

> *"Supernatural cannot mean anything except supremely real, fully in conformity with the conditions which nature imposes on beings."*
>
> —TEILHARD DE CHARDIN, *HOW I BELIEVE*

Humanism, originating in the Renaissance, is a philosophy that bases values on the best potential of human beings rather than on supernatural causes or the teachings of religious authority. It includes libertarian respect for rights, concern for those in need, commitment to equality, acting responsibly and honestly toward others, civil-mindedness, and making a contribution to humanity through personally fulfilling work.

In *Religions, Values, and Peak-Experiences*, Abraham Maslow presents the humanist response to the traditional view of the supernatural/transcendent, when he writes: "It is very likely, indeed almost certain, that these older reports, phrased in terms of supernatural revelation, were, in fact, perfectly natural, human peak-experiences of the kind that can easily be examined today, which, however, were phrased in terms of whatever conceptual, cultural, and linguistic framework the particular seer had available in his time."

Maslow's statement shows the difference between secular humanism and humanistic religion. In humanism, the inherent potential in people is the final reality. In religious faith with a humanist orientation, there is More, something above and beyond the natural, i.e., supernatural, that transcends our human powers and endows us with grace. This grace widens our love, wisdom, and healing power. From the religious point of view, pure humanism does not go far enough and can fall prey to hubris. This is the belief that all achievement results from human effort. It is a denial of the need for transcendent support, the arrogance of *ego*: "Edging God Out."

We can refuse to divide reality into the merely humanist-natural and the totally supernatural. German theologian Karl Rahner used the term "supernatural existential" to refer to the presence of the transcendent in all appearances, not only in the obviously numinous ones. This is reminiscent of the implicate order beneath the explicate order described by David Bohm. Ken Wilber adds: "Supernatural is simply the next *natural* step in overall or higher development and evolution."

In the spiritually facilitating religious view, the supernatural, the More than natural, is an existential reality in us. Then faith experience is not an add-on. It is a way to contact our spiritual identity, the often unconscious part of us that easily rises into consciousness as we become open to it and as we engage in spiritual practices. It transcends the humanist credo because it enjoins universal love among us and a divine love toward us. Our authentic self is then the same as that of the divine, love.

Faith can help us know the More that is our authentic self. This does not happen by our own ego effort but comes to us as a gift. Such grace is another example of the More. Indeed, grace is intrinsic to our very being since it is the point of contact between ordinary life and the transcendent, a rendezvous we were born to show up for. A student of mine reported that one time she was tired at her boring job and looked out the window at horses standing quietly in a pasture. She immediately heard a voice inside her say: "*That* is your real self." This is an example both of how grace comes to us and how an immediate reality in nature mediates a revelation of the transcendent.

Religion conditions us into the possibility of combining polarities and opposites. This accounts for how we can see our powerlessness and have the faith to believe that a higher power will help us. Wholeness is both a psychological and spiritual enterprise. It is in us fully already and not yet. This means that it is both our heritage and our work. Psychology and spirituality each offer tools to help us do that work. A religion that is psychologically sane in its concepts and spiritually trustworthy in its challenges is useful in the marvelous enterprise of activating the wholeness that we are. Then nonduality extends to the distinctions between psychological and spiritual, religious and spiritual.

> *"God is more intimate to me than my innermost*
> *being and higher than my highest being."*
>
> —ST. AUGUSTINE

Three More Ways of Describing the Divine

"How you like infinity disclosed is
a matter of taste really."

—DAVID DEIDA

The two traditional configurations of God—as transcendent and immanent—are also reflected in mysticism, depth psychology, and the evolution of consciousness view, three more ways of approximating what the divine may mean.

A Mystical View

We find an example of God as More in *mysticism*. Mystics usually follow what is called the apophatic path. This refers to a letting go of attempts to know God through teachings about God. Conceptual thought cannot describe what is ineffable. Mystics experience a realization that is More than what theological or ecclesiastical authorities may say about who God is. Their understanding of the divine favors personal intuition rather than adherence to a creed, and what follows is an unbrokered relationship to God.

This is a subversive and enormously liberating belief about what faith is, since it subjects authority and tradition to the inner voice of the individual and subjects abstract theory to practical experience. In the book of Job we read a description of the primacy of experience in mystical consciousness: "I had heard of you by the hearing of the ear, but now my eye sees you" (42:5).

William James, in *The Varieties of Religious Experience*, wrote: "Mystical states seem to those who experience them to be also states of knowledge. They are states of insight into depths of truth unplumbed by the discursive intellect. As a rule they carry with them a curious sense of authority. . . ." This authority of experience is central to mysticism—and an essential feature of adulthood too. It stands in opposition to hierarchal churches that insist their adherents follow their view of divine revelation in precisely the ways they formulate them.

Mysticism in all traditions has in common a realization that the divine, the natural, and the human are three aspects of one single reality. A mystic nonetheless does not become lost in a diffuse oceanic state of unity, but rather lets go of any sense of a separate existence while his conventional identity nonetheless remains intact. A mystic says: "I want to enjoy the taste of melon but not become a melon because then I have lost the experience."

Mystical experience is thus considered psychologically legitimate since it does not muddle our identity but stabilizes and enlivens it in new directions. It opens imagination. It does not blur our boundaries but shows us how porous they are.

There is an organic dimension too. Neuroscientists from the University of California at San Diego located cells in the frontal lobe that become active in mystical/religious experiences. They studied epileptic patients who have what seem to be mystical experiences during seizures. The seizures stimulate a collection of cells in the frontal lobe. A similar reaction occurs in the general population when they are shown symbols of their religious beliefs or affiliations. Thus a neurological basis for spiritual experience has been proposed by biologists. Richard Harris, bishop of Oxford, wrote: "It would not be surprising if God had created us with a physical facility for belief." Sociologists further realize that religious belief serves a useful social function, to keep the forces of greed and hate at bay, a form of crowd control.

The complement to the apophatic path is the cataphatic path of knowledge, using intellect and imagination to understand the divine. This is the more common style in both the transcendent and immanent views. The cataphatic is not the opposite of the apophatic. Usually people interested in religion begin with a cataphatic style and then move to the apophatic, which does not deny the usefulness of the former but simply extends and transcends it. We attempt to learn and then open to experience beyond what can be learned. This is how faith keeps seeking understanding and understanding keeps bumping up against mystery and becomes so absorbed in it, so full of wonder at it, that it is content with the More than can be known.

The Depth View

In the *depth psychological* perspective, mainly represented by the work of Carl Jung, the accent is on God as immanent, but not as a reality dwelling deep within us as in the strictly theistic view. Here the immanence of the divine means that the depth of ourselves and of the universe *is* what we mean by God. Immanence is not God within but rather the within is God.

Jung's research and experience with patients led him to believe in the spiritual dimension of the psyche. He noticed that religious language preserved and presented this fact. Jung's depth psychology recasts the insights of revelation from religion and myth as the immemorial and enduring intuitions of our collective humanity. The faith challenge from the perspective of depth psychology is to see the synonymy between what comes to us in dreams, synchronicities, and myths and what comes as religious revelation.

Here is an example of how a religious teaching is perceived in a depth perspective: the church, over the centuries, taught that the bread and wine in the Eucharist are the body and blood of Christ/God. From the depth psychology perspective this longstanding insistence held a grand mystical realization that the divine resides in things, all things, and in us too. The theology of the Eucharist securely held that message for two thousand years and now—thanks to Pierre Teilhard de Chardin, Jung, and the new cosmology—we see its full implications: like the Eucharist, we and nature too are sacraments, outward tangible signs of an inner divine reality.

We have finally placed the Eucharist in the monstrance of the universe, where it indeed deserves perpetual adoration. This can also explain why so many people kept believing in the theology of the Eucharist. It was preserving a truth about our deep-down identity.

Thus in the depth view, "God" is a way of describing the essential reality of who we are and what everything is, all one and the same. God, from this perspective, is usually an intrapsychic reality, as is all our knowledge, perception, and experience. In this context, God is who we are, real, but not discrete in the way externally existing objects are real. The higher Self/God is real instead in the way that love, beauty, vitality, and musical harmonies are real.

In this view, there may be no God as a person who is transcendent, but there is a God archetype, the center of the psyche, the higher Self. This Self is much more than what we would ordinarily refer to as a "person."

The phrase "higher Self" is another spatial metaphor that points to a potential to transcend circumstances, time, or place. "Higher" means higher than ego can reach, higher than the givens of life can affect, and higher than can be fully known by the intellect. This way of referring to transcendence keeps the focus on the "More" dimension of ourselves and the universe. Gerard Manley Hopkins expressed it well in his poem "Spring and Fall":

> Nor mouth had, no nor mind, expressed
> What heart heard of, ghost guessed. . . .

> To accept the fact, or rather presence, of tran-
> scendence in all that is requires us to abandon our
> limited way of perceiving, i.e., accepting as real
> only what can be demonstrated. That is the chal-
> lenge religion and depth psychology accept. We do
> not have to be religious to accept it, only open to

a knowledge that is not limited to the logical and scientifically provable.

Depth psychology helps us in that project because it finds truth in the unconscious, that which is unknown to us but strongly affecting our lives, motivations, choices, and perceptions. The unconscious is free from the limitations of the conscious mind. For instance, in the unconscious, all time is simultaneous while in the conscious mind, we live entirely in the present with thoughts of what may be, which we call the future, and thoughts of what has been, which we call the past. Unconscious forces lobby for our vote. Our conscious choices are our votes.

Thus nothing is old or new in the unconscious, but everything is happening now. The Exodus of the Israelites from Egypt happened long ago from the historical perspective of the conscious mind. In the unconscious it is as real now as it was then and as current as our getting up this morning. We can see how the style of the unconscious is the style of religious meanings. Faith does what the unconscious does, brings the past into the present and integrates the two.

Often depth psychology makes the exact same declaration that conventional religion does but in different language. God and divine powers are archetypes in depth psychology. Yet God is believed to come to our aid when all else fails. This can especially happen when we are powerless to help ourselves. For instance in the first step of the Alcoholics Anonymous program, we admit we are powerless to manage our lives and by the third step we trust that God will restore us to sane living.

In the archetype of the heroic journey, the hero engages in derring-do and often conquers his foe. But the time comes when he is wounded and disabled from taking action. That will lead to a visit from an assisting force archetype, the equivalent of the helper-God in religious parlance. Robin

Hood in prison needed Maid Marian's aid to save him from being hanged. Pinocchio is spit out by the whale and washed up on the shore, inanimate and water-logged. That moment of powerlessness evokes the Blue Fairy, symbol of the transcendent, to come to his aid to make him a real boy.

In religion and in depth psychology alike, the aid of God or of the assisting force comes to us by grace. This is a free gift to us *in our weakest moment, so we can know incontrovertibly that it is not the result of our efforts.* "For power is made perfect in weakness" (2 Cor 12:9). Likewise, we feel the grace to be arising from a transcendent source, so it feels like a *personal presence* in our lives: "*Thou* art with me."

Another similarity is in the fact that in both instances the hero feels gratitude rather than accomplishment, another sign it is about grace, not effort. The same theme appears in our existential predicaments as we read in the quotation below from French sociologist Emile Durkheim, using neither religious nor psychological terms!

> When this ultimate crisis comes . . .when there is no way out, that is the very moment when we explode from within and the totally other emerges. . . . It is the sudden surfacing of a strength, a security of unknown origin, welling up from beyond reason, rational expectation, or hope.

An Evolutionary View

A fox is a perfect fox in this moment, having developed from embryo to adulthood in accord with a fixed inner plan, a genetic entelechy or the blueprint of foxness. This is being. The entire fox species is nevertheless evolving each day to survive better than ever for the future. This is becoming. Both are happening in every moment. Thus everything is evolving so there is no static final version of anything. All things—and people—are developing into what best accommodates the givens of their lives and gives them the strength to handle ever-changing challenges. Though everything is already blueprinted, yet new and better spin-offs are continually appearing.

At this moment, foxes are becoming more equipped to live in their environment. In this sense, they are still being created. Creation, in the evolutionary perspective, is not a once and for all event but an ongoing project, with development and evolution as its operating principles. Everything is continually transcending what it is now so it can be More. This is how it fulfills its inherent design and progresses. For foxes this has to do with survival in the wild and more effective caring for their young. For us it has to do with fulfilling our More, our potential for personal and universal love, enlightened wisdom, and healing power. A religion contributes to our evolution when it recommends and fosters those virtues.

Since everything is evolving, all is fearlessly and ineluctably future-oriented. In the evolutionary view, God can be the name of that orientation, the future we are aimed toward. We are, in that sense, all moving toward God when we live in openness to what next will bud in the evolutionary pageant. That energy exists in us as an ineradicable urge to fulfill our own unique potential for becoming, what turns out to be the same as the emergence of the divine in human history.

To find God is not only to look within but to look into the future, where the More-than-is-now is being revealed. The future is the activation of the infinite potential in us and everything. To trust that as a truth, no matter what happens to dissuade or discourage us about it, is faith, a belief in the future of an evolved universe. A faith commitment is a pledge to join that project as co-creators.

A simple way to understand the power of the future in human consciousness is to consider ideals. They are standards we do not have now but to which we aspire. The ideal is what is hidden potentially in the real, waiting to be actualized.

This is a need in us and in all things. We have a driving force in us to become more than we are. Our entelechy is naturally evolutionary.

The only way we know we are free is that we act against our default shadow setting of greed, hate, and ignorance even to the point of risking our lives to maintain integrity. We can also transcend the natural primary instinct for survival. That is the More of self-sacrifice. This helps us understand the religious theme of sacrifice: We give up what our ego is attached to for something More. We surrender ourselves to a force that seems beyond us but wells up from within us.

Religion keeps a vocabulary alive that no other science preserves or even recognizes, except depth psychology. Words like "sacrifice," "resurrection," "ascension," "incarnation," and "epiphany" are examples of common motifs in religion but also in the story of our human journey. Each of these archetypes represents an *evolutionary possibility* within the human psyche. Each is a promise of what humans can become in the full flowering of conscious evolution. Religion has preserved all these over the centuries, but applied them to gods and saints. Thanks to modern theology we realize these are callings to all of us, in the entelechy of each of us in unique ways. Thanks to the evolutionary approach, we know the archetypes are descriptors of possibilities in human nature and in the natural world that are waiting for full flowering. Religion was preserving the best information about us in its theology. Mythology was doing the same in myth and story. Now depth psychology does the same.

Religion is a response to the universal experience of the sacred that happens in an evolutionary cultural-historical context. Anyone can respond, whether or not she is a member of an institutional religion. The unconscious depth dimension of the psyche is our uniquely human and utterly suitable pathway to the numinous. This consciousness is possible in any religion. The evolutionary approach to consciousness does not degrade or depreciate any religion, its history, and its continual multiplication into many traditions and sects. We evolve best as we *transcend* and *include* the past rather than cancel or repudiate it.

The monastic life as described by Thomas Merton included Buddhist practices. In fact, he described himself as "a Buddhist Catholic and a Catholic Buddhist." We see an interweaving of many spiritual practices in most non-fundamentalist traditions today. This openness transcends compulsive ties to one's own tradition as sufficient and acknowledges the value of our long history of evolution toward becoming better humans.

> *"Our new sense of the universe is itself a type of revelatory experience. Presently we are moving . . . to a new comprehensive context for all religions. . . . The natural world is itself the primary . . . presence of the sacred, the primary moral value. . . . The human community becomes sacred through its participation in the larger planetary community."*
>
> —THOMAS BERRY

Chapter Seven

Mystery and Metaphor

*"He left unobscured the vast
darkness of the subject."*

—ALFRED NORTH WHITEHEAD
COMPLIMENTING BERTRAND RUSSELL

Mystery is no longer a word used only in religious circles. Today science seems to be realizing that there is an implacable and intriguing mystery in the world of physics. It is a rare person who still believes that someday everything will be understood fully. Niels Bohr expressed this well: "When it comes to atoms, language can be used only as in poetry." We can know the world only through metaphor and analogy. With regard to knowledge, this makes science and religion very much alike. The incomprehensible is the ultimate subject of art, poetry, religion, and science too. This is another example of how our human search for understanding will always be a form of fishing, not a final catch.

"God" is a metaphor for a mystery that cannot be defined, especially not in words. A mystery in this context is not a whodunit or a puzzle but a reality too profound and cryptic to be comprehended fully. We can distinguish two kinds of metaphors, literary and approximating. For an adult in faith, religious events and symbols are not metaphorical in the literary sense, simple comparisons, but approximating a mystery too deep for—transcendent of—words or images. Such metaphors are not thought up in the intellect as literary metaphors are. They are not literary devices. To an adult in faith, they are rich revelations, clues to the divine—the hidden reality of who we really are and what the universe really is—no matter how unpromising the appearances seem. In that sense, the divine is the fulfillment and pinnacle of all that is.

Paul Tillich commented that anyone seeking meaning has religious faith. Metaphorical images are meaningful to us because, unlike thought, they touch upon all areas of our being: mind, heart, feeling, intuition, imagination. Plato in his *Symposium* says that Eros is the child of poverty and plenty. Our lively feelings are born from our limited capacities of mind as well as the abundance always awaiting discovery.

Symballein in Greek means to join together. *Symbolon* refers to a sign or token of an agreement. In ancient times, when two people made a contract, they divided a bone or a coin in two. One person carried half as a pledge of something owed to the person holding the other half. Each piece thus represented, but was not, a whole. Both halves were needed for the full meaning and fulfillment of the contract. This is precisely how a symbol functions. One half is in the obvious reality, in our pocket, and the other half is in mystery, somewhere beyond us. This is reminiscent of Plato's *Symposium*, in which humans are compared to halves that pursue one another to form relationships that complete them. Our longings for God correspond to an inner fact about us, the reality of More, archetype of the higher Self.

The early Greek philosopher Thales asserted that the gods were everywhere, not only on Mount Olympus. Theagenes of Rhegium, in the sixth century B.C., considered the names of the gods as representative of our human faculties or of elements in nature. The Stoic philosophers saw the gods as allegorical and as personifications of natural forces. This perspective was widely accepted by educated Romans and Greeks. The Stoic Chrysippus in the first century A.D.

proposed that the gods were physical or ethical principles, not persons. Musonius Rufus, a Stoic teacher who influenced Marcus Aurelius, taught that the gods were elements of nature. He believed that all the gods are part of one cosmic order and that there is only one single divinity.

By late antiquity, no cultured person took the existence of the gods literally. The psyche had succeeded in liberating itself from literalism (idolatry) *while preserving a belief in divinity.* That is symbolic of how any of us can reclaim the riches of religion while maintaining our intelligence and sophistication. A living metaphor is the best bridge toward that possibility.

The style of believing that the divine is "merely" or "nothing but" allegory, rather than More, is reminiscent of Euhemerism. This was a theory of Sicilian-Greek philosopher Euhemeros, 315 B.C. He taught that the gods were originally actual human heroes who were later apotheosized. He also taught that divinities were only metaphors of human powers with no transcendent existence: "The gods are merely reflections of our own human nature." This more extreme view was dubbed atheistic by conservatives. For instance, Cicero wrote: "Euhemeros has portrayed the deaths and burials of the gods. Does he seem to have provided a factual base for religion or has he actually removed the need for it?" (Cicero, *De Natura Deorum* I: 42). We notice that the metaphorical approach to theological affirmations is considered suspect in that same way today by fundamentalists.

Advances in science that seem to eliminate the role or need for religion also make for suspicion among strictly orthodox believers. For instance, the physician Hippocrates affirmed that mental dysfunction was an illness rather than something caused by the gods. For that, he might have been thought of as irreverent. Benjamin Franklin was condemned by the religious fundamentalists of his day when he invented the lightning rod. They said that it denied God the chance to punish evildoers by striking them dead with a bolt from above. A possessiveness about divine explanations for disaster is certainly an unfortunate style among religious institutions that want to maintain their importance and control. As long as religion is about that rather than about how to advance in wisdom and to love more, it will always be distrusted by healthy humans.

Mature religious faith sees doctrines as metaphors that come close to portraying the deeper meanings in life. Thus a hyacinth blooming in springtime is an ancient symbol of new life. This is a metaphor approximating the richness of renewal of which the earth is capable and so far has always fulfilled. The hyacinth can be an image that forecasts human destiny for eternal aliveness. In fact, pollens of hyacinths have been found in prehistoric burial sites. This flower is a longstanding symbol of the collective destiny of the universe to rise into its full capacity for light. It thus becomes, through metaphor, much more puissant in human consciousness than the flower hyacinth as a fact of botany. The symbol of the hyacinth can go the next step into access to the divine, as the sustaining power of life over death. In every instance, religious symbolism reflects transcendent implications of nature, transparent, by its beauty alone, to a transcendent source. These lines from two poets set ablaze this deeper appreciation of metaphor:

> "Earth's crammed with heaven,
> And every common bush afire with God. . . ."

> —ELIZABETH BARRETT BROWNING, "AURORA LEIGH"

> ". . . I have felt
> A presence that . . .
> Rolls through all things."

> —WILLIAM WORDSWORTH, "TINTERN ABBEY"

Are There Atheists?

"There is no evidence for the non-existence of
God. You simply have to accept this on faith."

—WOODY ALLEN

Once God is the ground of being and the ultimate concern for meaning, as theologian Paul Tillich would have it, most of us have faith. Then there is no full-on atheism or total secularism. Our universal and enduring longing for meaning in life and nature faces us and all society Godward. Carl Jung wrote: "Consciousness, continually in danger of being led astray by its own light, of becoming a rootless will o' the wisp, longs for the healing power of nature, for the deep wells of being and for unconscious communion with life in all its countless forms."

When people say they are atheists, they may mean they cannot accept the existence of a transcendent God, especially not as a person who rescues the innocent—about which history demonstrates continual disappointment. Some people become atheists because they cannot reconcile a providential God and the suffering of the innocent. This implies that God should be intervening in injustice or else there is no God.

However, once God is not a being but the being of all beings, we may say that God is no longer a moral or immoral agent but a depth presence in all that is. Then the problem of evil in the world takes on a new cast. The question is not why God allows evil but why humans so often choose it, especially when we are free to make choices for justice, love, and peace. So many of us persecute others rather than rescue them. Shakespeare laments in *Othello*: "Do deeds to make heaven weep, all earth amazed [struck dumb with horror]."

Alfred North Whitehead in *Process and Reality* mentions the "brief Galilean vision of humility that flickered throughout the ages, uncertainly." He contrasts this with the view that won out in which God is a Caesar. God in the image of the inflated ego and as a projection of ego gives us permission to hate and to punish.

The word "God" sounds male and distant, heavy with fearsome connotations from our past, such as stern reprimand and punitive threat. Yet God may also be viewed as kindly disposed toward us when God is the wholeness in us, the light in us and in all things. Franciscan theologian St. Bonaventure says: "God's power is his humility. God's strength is his weakness. God's greatness is his lowliness." Thus a commitment to find redemption through suffering and by surrendering to the givens of life may bring us closer to the mystery of who God is.

German Lutheran theologian Jürgen Moltmann writes: "Creation is not a demonstration of God's boundless power but a communication of his love." Studies show that self-esteem is higher when a person has a kindly image of God. Those with low self-esteem see God as punitive. To look at the other side of this finding, it seems clear that a God who is love is in the best interests of human health!

In the course of religious history, many mystics of all traditions have agreed that this most accurately reflects the underlying nature of reality, a way of saying we are in a friendly universe. The mystics affirmed that the divine light can be contacted directly in our souls. Making such contact with the light, which might be called God, can be our true human fulfillment. Glowing in the dark can turn out to be a life purpose and the foundation of our joy.

It may be easier to believe in God when God is configured this way: Something, we know not what, is always and everywhere wisely and lovingly at work, we know not how, to make the world more than it is yet, to make us more than we are now. This loving intent is what is known as the divine. It is simultaneously the life force of nature, the heart of the universe, and our own lively energy.

Faith is shown by our response to the four elements of religion and spirituality—belief, morality, ritual, devotion. Curiously, this response may be common to many people, even those who style themselves atheists. Recently I was discussing this with a friend who declares herself to be a confirmed atheist. She mentioned that she *does* believe that there is something going on in the universe that is not willed by humans or that seems to have an orderly and an evolutionary direction. She called this the Tao. I proposed that this was a way of referring to the transcendent, that which is beyond ego and intellect.

In addition, she follows a moral code in her daily life. I have also noticed over the years that she will engage in rituals, though not specifically religious ones. Finally, she does not show devotion to any god or saint, but she has an admirable devotion to nature, which is one way that religious devotion is expressed, more and more nowadays. Thus all four elements are present in her life. Even the name she chose for herself refers to the transcendent: Angela.

To give her a full hearing, I add this note from her to me:

> I think that the project of a consciously developing human is to attend to the world itself, to dwell with the elements of all that is here, and to be ever aware of the way one acts toward all that is here. This, in my view, tends to ground us in the virtues of humility, forbearance, wonder, reverence, gratitude, amazement, and all the other celebrated attributes of a conscious, well-formed person. Our agency within this world then becomes the bedrock of our morality. It is forged here in our attentiveness and in our wrestling with our responsibilities, limits, and rights, rather than being superimposed by fiat or by some constructed notion of a deity's commandments. Thus there is no room for "the devil made me do it" or

"It is God's will, not mine" and similar excuses for
bad behavior and a lazy life. There is no easy dis-
pensation and no indulgences come from above.

How We Might Take God Personally

The *Isha Upanishad* states: "That supreme Person abiding
in the very heart of life am I." In this sense, God is personal
because we are. Theologian Denis Edwards writes: "God can
be seen as the immanent power of becoming who enables this
kind of life-bearing universe to emerge." God is then personal
in the sense that personal denotes *conscious*, not in the sense
of separate and distinct the way individual humans are. Paul
Tillich adds: "God is not a person but not less than a person."

The ego is afraid of uncertainty. Numinosity, a mysterious power that suggests the presence of the divine, is disturbing to the ego because it is beyond—transcends—its control.
Yet, the spiritual journey often begins with the realization—
not just as information but as interior conviction—that there
is a higher power than ego. As we have been seeing so far, the
belief that there is "More" can be a belief in God without ever
using that word. The More is the transcendent in reality, the
divine in people and things, the essential and inextinguish-
able light in all that is. For an adult in faith, it shows up in our
experience as grace, a special moment of wisdom or strength
that makes us feel accompanied on life's journey.

We keep noticing that themes, such as that of an accompanying presence that loves us personally, are not limited to
one religious tradition but appear over and over in many traditions. This is a sign that we are in a larger realm than that
of wish and fantasy. Universal themes seem to show us that
we are in contact with the components of our deepest psyche
and the wisdom of our collective humanity.

When our own experience mirrors archetypal themes,
they certainly feel true to us. For instance, our sense of a

divine presence in our lives may *feel like* being personally loved, whether or not our rational mind concurs. Adults can be comfortable with that style of relationship-faith. It is a relationship because of our sense of being loved. It is faith because it is a mystery that transcends explanation yet cannot be denied as a personal experience.

The guardian angel is a common figure in monotheistic religions. A look at this archetype helps us understand the personal and accompanying dimension of God in adult faith. A guardian angel has personal implications since each of us is believed to have one of our own. In the *Phaedo* by Plato we find a similar reference: "We each have an accompanying spirit" (108b). We hear Socrates say: "I, too, believe that the gods are our guardians, and that we are a possession of theirs." Likewise, the Buddha of compassion, Avalokitesvara, "hears the cries of all who suffer" and comes to the aid of each in a unique way. In the Native American tradition, we see many references to invisible animal companions as guardians.

In the journey of faith, we might believe in a literal guardian angel at first but later we see it as a personification of transcendent support, the archetype of grace, that assists us on our life path. Religion appreciates these archetypes but can make them seem literal, especially to encourage devotion. As we grow in faith we move from literal to metaphorical, from a superficial configuration to a deep appreciation of the reality of who we are and how the world is constructed.

When we stopped believing literally, some of our relatives might have thought we had lost our faith. In reality, we found it. Our faith, like our bodies, simply grew up. This happens to us, regarding the guardian angels, when we delve deeply into the religious truth they represent. Then we might still be able to maintain a personal and devotional sense about them too. Archetypes and metaphors do not cancel faith; they enrich it.

We can use this discussion of guardian angels to revisit an important theme in this book: When our religion inculcated a belief in guardian angels, it somehow felt right. This is because it fit as a personification of an archetype we all carry, the assisting force that aids and guards the hero. We could live with and appreciate that spiritual force all our adult lives without having to keep believing there was a literal guardian angel assigned to us. Later, we might have believed that our loved ones who died might still be watching over us. Now we could expand the guardian angel concept to fit our ancestors or friends.

Here is an example from Japanese Buddhism: Fugen Bosatsu was a Bodhisattva, an enlightened saint who chooses not to enter nirvana until he has helped others find enlightenment too. Fugen is a Bodhisattva of wisdom. This means he represents the kind of wisdom and caring that resides in the Buddha nature in all of us. He is described as one who waits for us until we choose to let go of ignorance. Fugen's intuition about our ignorance is so profound that he compassionately understands the touching motives behind all human choices, no matter how bad they may be. His commitment to this contemplation of our predicament mirrors his commitment not to judge others but to aid them. He might be called a Buddhist version of a guardian angel.

Fugen is not believed to be in a heaven realm at a distance from us, but is a living *depiction of what we can become* when our spiritual potential is activated. The image of Fugen sitting on a lotus upheld by white elephants is a metaphor for the grand and powerful support that is believed to be available to all of us once we awaken. Thus the person of Fugen is a metaphor for spiritual support, and the image of him is a metaphor for how we receive that support. This support is not in the sky above us but in the sky within us. There, or rather here, is a beatific vision of a pantheon of assisting forces that appear in images as helper angels and saints.

Once the images are recognized as deeply real but not literal fact, we have entered the world of adult faith.

In human relationships it takes two to say yes but only one to say no. In the relationship of God to humans, it takes only one to say yes because God does not only accompany us. In the realm of faith, God pursues us and loves us no matter how much we say no, the equivalent of Fugen's compassion for our ignorance and his waiting for us to come back. The same theme appears in Christianity in the Sacred Heart of Jesus. In all these images we are looking at a mystical faith-intuition about the nature of the divine and *how it can feel personal.* It is a comforting comment on how God loves, that is, how love happens personally. It is unconditional, so a phrase like "God is love" says more about our human identity than our driver's license ever can. This is how faith can be an aid to the full appreciation of what the human story is about.

In Christian iconography, Michelangelo's *Pietà* shows Mary holding the dead body of Jesus at the foot of the cross. She sits for the portrait of our universal human archetype of grief in response to an unjust death. (Every death of one's child feels unjust indeed.) Object relations theorist Margaret Mahler calls the holding behavior of a mother "the midwife of individuation, of psychological birth." Thus from an archetypal perspective, in the *Pietà* Mary, mother of the infant Jesus, is the midwife to resurrection, the full birth of the adult Christ. This is a proclamation that life can come from death when the divine feminine embraces us. These are metaphors, not taken literally in adult religious consciousness because they are too rich to be so limited. Might they not also, however, be the secret energies in our humanity, actually more true than any literality can conjure or imagine? Religious revelation is then an attempt to tell that fact-defying secret, or rather, good news. Faith is a yes to it.

God and Evil

One of the most persistent issues concerning belief in God is the problem of evil. For many, ancient Greek philosopher Epicurus's argument still holds up:

> Is God willing to prevent evil, but not able?
> *Then he is not omnipotent.*
>
> Is he able, but not willing?
> *Then he is malevolent.*
>
> Is he both able and willing?
> *Then why is there evil?*
>
> Is he neither able nor willing?
> *Then why call him God?*

When God is configured as a rescuer, the question of why he permits suffering is unanswerable. If God is immanent love, then suffering becomes part of how God exists, as a sharer in our painful story. In the *Gitagovinda* by Jayadeva, Radha, lover of Krishna, is suffering because of his desertion of her. This grief is precisely what readies her to become the true bride of his divine love. The power of her longing is what draws Krishna to come back to her and share in her suffering. We notice in the Hindu tradition too, that God is configured as sharing human suffering. In the story of Radha, we see the archetypal power of our pain to draw the divine to us.

The question: "Why do the innocent suffer?" hails from the superstition that goodness will inevitably be rewarded and evil punished. This is a mean-spirited view. True love would want the good to be happy and the evil to be converted to goodness so they could be happy too. That is mature loving, the only legitimate love in a religion in which God is said to be love.

The God who is transcendent, the author of the givens of life, does not promise this. Nor does the immanent God who is present within the givens of life. *For an adult, suffering is not a punishment and happiness is not a reward.* Then the sense of who God is follows suit and natural disasters do not indicate that there is no God or that God punishes. They show only that we do not understand the divine when we configure God as a rescuer, rewarder, or punisher. An adult does not believe in a God like that, and such a belief would contradict the givens of life rather than enlighten us about them.

The Bible offers at least five explanations of evil and the suffering it causes. The first is in Genesis, which shows that suffering can be the occasion of God's mercy. Evil can be redemptive because God brings good out of evil. Joseph says to his brothers: "Even though you intended to do harm to me, God intended it for good" (50:20). In a wider vision, the turning-into-good is God-in-events. Thomas Jefferson in a letter to Benjamin Rush seems to describe this tradition when he writes: "When great evils happen, I am in the habit of looking out for what good may arise from them as consolations to us, and Providence has in fact so established the order of things, as that most evils are the means of producing some good."

A second biblical view is in the wisdom tradition. Here evil is inevitable, a given that cannot stop us from choosing to be good in any case. Life has meaning but not predictability. No matter how firm our faith may be, we are not immune to suffering. Suffering is then not caused by sin, only inherent in nature and in the human story. This is the ultimate realization in the book of Job.

A third biblical view of evil is found in Ecclesiastes. This book is not in the wisdom tradition since it does not portray life as meaningful. "Vanity of vanities" is its most famous quotation. That word in Hebrew is *hevel*, meaning vacuity, absurdity, uselessness, literally a fleeting mist, utterly ephemeral. This word is used thirty times in the book. The philosophy of Ecclesiastes is that evil is here to stay, that we cannot eliminate it, and that our best bet is to enjoy what we can of life: "There is nothing better for people under the sun than to eat, and drink, and enjoy themselves, for this will go with them in their toil through the days of life that God gives them under the sun" (8:15).

A fourth view is in the prophetic tradition. Here it is sin, unjust deeds done by people that lead to evil. Our suffering is a consequence of misdeeds, a punishment for disobedience to God. This same theme is in the story of Adam and Eve in the first chapter of Genesis and is found throughout the Bible.

Suffering/evil was also seen by the prophets as originating in oppression from the outside as when the Syrians conquered Palestine from Egypt in 198 B.C. and persecuted the Jewish population there.

The prophet Amos in the eighth century spoke of social sin, not only personal sin. Thus to oppress the poor was also a sin leading to judgment as was standing by and watching it happen without intervening. In this view, people are called upon to take the action that people ask God to take. Seeing sin as social rather than only personal, by the way, is another example of how religion has contributed to helping us expand our consciences and consciousness.

A fifth view, apocalyptic, is found in the book of Daniel and climaxes in the book of Revelation: People suffer and evil happens now because the good are being attacked by invisible forces that are fiercer than humans can handle. St. Paul is in the apocalyptic tradition when he writes: "For our struggle is not against enemies of blood and flesh, but against the rulers, against the authorities, against the cosmic powers of this present darkness, against the spiritual forces of evil in the heavenly places" (Eph 6:12).

The apocalyptic view offers hope in the triumph of goodness at the end of time when angels will triumph over demons in a final battle. It also affirms and promises that the reign of evil is slated to end by the grace of God, not by human intervention.

The apocalyptic view captures the human imagination like no other. It appeals to the child in us since it offers a simple explanation, an exciting story, colorful demons and angels, our ultimate safety, punishment of others, a happy ending, and less pressure on us to make sure everything comes out right.

There are always doomsday prophets in this tradition who prey upon our childish fears and tell us when the world will end. They often choose a round number, another sign of superstition, e.g., 2012 or 2020. Adults in faith and spiritual consciousness do not believe in predictions about an Armageddon or world cataclysm. They are not at the mercy of fearmongering but live each day with integrity and then hope for the best.

We can compare the view of evil and suffering in the prophetic and apocalyptic traditions:

Origins of evil in the prophetic view	Origins of evil in the apocalyptic view
People violate divine law	Evil forces are at work in the world
Suffering is caused by God	Suffering is caused by demons opposed to God's laws
We are punished for our evil deeds	Evil automatically arises to oppose the light
Evil consequences can be ended by repentance	Good will triumph over evil
People are required to act if any change is to occur, and God will help them	God will intervene for people in the end times

Noticing Our Own Dark Side

Left to ourselves, merely as *Homo sapiens*, we might be headed for self-destruction. Relying only on what is innate in this gene pool gives humanity little hope for survival. For instance, though we have an inherent primitive moral sense, we have a built-in *physical* survival tendency toward retaliation. Science shows that, for men, revenge lowers blood pressure after a stressful insult has led to a dangerous rise in adrenaline. Women's blood pressure, on the other hand, goes up when they are forced to retaliate.

Child psychologist Jean Piaget found that by six years old children believe that retaliatory punishment will be the inevitable and automatic consequence of misconduct. This makes it easy to believe there is a God who does the same. We become sure that God will punish us for our transgressions. This illusion disappears by puberty. We begin to believe we can get away with things sometimes.

Retaliation is an example of one of humanity's default settings. A mature religious and spiritual consciousness will see loving-kindness and restorative justice as more powerful than retribution. An adult with faith has chosen that practice no matter what the crime or how the givens play out. In addition, to the person of faith it is not that we have virtue but that God manifests virtue through us when we are open and willing: "For those who live according to the flesh set their minds on the things of the flesh, but those who live according to the Spirit set their minds on the things of the Spirit" (Rom 8:5).

Without religion we might have nothing to call upon as resources in how to be with others except our Cro-Magnon genetic code. It includes retaliating though it includes our rescuing victims too. It is certainly not a large enough toolbox to open our whole potential for love or to create a peaceful world. For that we need the voices of the prophets who came to show us an alternative path: Buddha, Christ, Gandhi,

Martin Luther King Jr., Dorothy Day, the Dalai Lama, and a vast host of saints and heroes who taught nonviolent loving-kindness by word and example.

Carl Jung alluded to the proclivity in our human heritage toward evil as the negative collective shadow. It seems, from a glance at history, that the human community has a built-in set of negative inclinations. They include:

War

Torture

Genocide

Slavery

Hate crimes, based on bigotry and scapegoating because of race, nationality, religion, political beliefs, social status, sexual orientation, or gender

Religion has examples of all these in its history. In its dominating form, religion has led to abuse of human freedom, intolerance, hate, and war. But in its positive facilitating form it is an integrative force in personality and society and contributes to basic trust in a cosmic orderliness.

It is telling that these five horrors are not listed in *The Diagnostic and Statistical Manual of Mental Disorders*. Psychiatric intervention is required if someone tortures animals but not if someone tortures humans. In fact, the American Psychological Association approved of torture. This is an example of how the psychological world works hand-in-glove with the purposes of the state. In that sense, it is like so many institutional religions. One is not insane if he practices torture as long as he is doing it as part of a governmental system. Psychological assistance is only about helping him beforehand to be able to carry it out without becoming too stressed by it or afterwards in the form of being debriefed from it. The same applies to war, another insane pastime that is not recognized as pathology in the *Manual*.

Faith in humanity is believing that though the five dark behaviors have often been our collective choices so far in history, our inclination toward destruction can be deactivated more and more, though probably not entirely. In the spiritually enlightened view, the shadow is not indelible. It is only a potential, a probability, and does not have to become an activity. That is our choice and we can change the way it is, as happened with the overturning of the prohibition against women's suffrage. In fact, light can come from the shadow since opposites constellate so easily in the psyche. John Milton expresses this in *Paradise Lost*, Book VII: "Orient light exhaling first from darkness. . . ."

I use the word "dark" not as referring literally to those who are dark in complexion but as a metaphor of that which is hidden and unacknowledged in us and thus can be dangerous because it is unconscious. The opposite of dark is not white but light.

The shadow is not our fate but our challenge. At the same time, an adult acknowledges the givens of life, which include an indelible appetite in the human species to engage in the five depraved abuses listed above. In that sense, there will always be a collective negative shadow side to us, but we can be less and less at the mercy of it. The path to this strength is in acknowledging our vulnerability to it and in our taking personal responsibility for it. The danger is in how we project our own shadow onto others. We befriend the negative shadow in ourselves when we accept its presence in us but choose not to act on it.

Also, we do not have to make choices to join in collective evils or stand by without speaking up against them. Every one of us is predisposed to enter the service of aggression, a default setting of surviving. This is why a spiritual practice is so necessary. Without the motivation to do good that comes from kindly common sense, spirituality, or religion, we are sitting ducks for the collective dark side to overtake us. Unfortunately, religion has too often been the agent of the shadow rather than its opponent. If religion is man-made, it has some good in it since that is a reliable trait of our humanity. If it is God-made, then it is good. However, we may have subverted that goodness by our man-made greed, hate, and ignorance—the Buddhist descriptors of the *negative* collective shadow.

There is also a *positive* collective shadow, the untapped potential for goodness that many heroic people have indeed tapped into and dedicated themselves to:

Commitment to liberty and self-determination

Nonviolent resistance of evil

Heroic self-sacrifice

Unstinting generosity

Unconditional, unreserved, and unbiased love and compassion: the capacity and willingness to negotiate, forgive, and reconcile, acknowledging the ultimate goodness in all persons

We can commit ourselves to following these avenues, which save us from being lost in the dark. The five dark choices are how we create hell on earth. The choices for the light are how we create heaven on earth. We wonder how God can create a hell, but it is we who do so. We say we want to go to heaven, but we so rarely take the opportunity to make it happen here in our world. We are indeed mysterious beings, but hope remains, "a thing with feathers that perches in the soul," as Emily Dickinson writes. There will never be no darkness, but there can be more and more light, thanks to the choices we can make.

Finally, we might wonder if God has a dark side too. To say that God is the depth reality of ourselves means that

God contains opposites, since that is a characteristic of our psyche. Thus God is light *and*, as poet Henry Vaughn wrote, "a deep and dazzling darkness" too. The Self combines opposites so it is dark and light, not only light, a mystery we cannot comprehend, but we can imagine or even experience. When we can't tolerate a combination of opposites in God, we split off the bad part and make it a literal Satan.

The Bible includes many examples of how people believed there was darkness in God. In every case they reflect the traits in the human ego when it is driven by hate or the compulsive need to control. In God's mantle, Elijah brutally slaughters the priests of Baal. In the book of Job, we meet a God who allows punishment of and cruelty toward an innocent man. We also notice passages like these: "Is a trumpet blown in a city, and the people are not afraid? Does disaster befall a city, unless the Lord has done it?" (Amos 3:6). "The Lord has made everything for its purpose, even the wicked for the day of trouble" (Prov 16:4). "I form light and create darkness, I make weal and create woe; I the Lord do all these things" (Isa 45:7). "On the way, at a place where they spent the night, the Lord met him and tried to kill him" (Exod 4:24). "And the Lord said, 'Who will entice Ahab, so that he may go up and fall at Ramoth-gilead?'" (1 Kings 22:20).

These quotations are not to be taken literally. They show us a God made in the image of the retaliatory ego. They refer to genuine evil, that is, evil with malicious or cruel intent. At the same time, the Bible presents God as someone reflecting the best possibilities in our higher Self: not giving up on others and not getting back at them. Thus we see light and dark in the biblical God. We also see suffering that God allows but, by the endurance of which, people grow. This is not evil as much as how the givens of life can hurt while they help us grow.

Equivalents in nature help us understand. Nature gives us earth in which to plant but also earthquakes, water to drink but also floods, breezes to cool us but also tornadoes.

This "dark side" is like the dark side of our own higher Self or God. It is painful, but ultimately it has an evolutionary and useful purpose. It is difficult but not malicious, as true evil is. This is reminiscent of how the givens of life are hard on us but also best for us.

The divine, the natural, and the human all contain both light and dark. These opposites can combine to become assisting forces on our journey if we use them that way. We do so when we say yes unconditionally to what is and make decisions that promulgate the light of wisdom and love. Then we say no courageously to evil and the whole world moves toward light too.

> *"Given human beings' love of truth, justice, peace, and freedom, creating a better, more compassionate world is a genuine possibility."*
>
> —DALAI LAMA

Befriending the Shadow through Loving-kindness

Loving, including universal loving, can be learned like any other skill. It happens when we look into our daily life for spiritual encouragement and opportunity. Tibetan teacher Sogyal Rinpoche wrote: "Spiritual practice is every person you meet and every unkind word you hear or which may be directed at you."

Buddha, like Christ and so many religious figures, suggested not giving up on others but appreciating their inherent goodness, as reliably in them as in us. His practice of loving-kindness helps this happen. In this practice we aspire to happiness, compassion, love, and equanimity for ourselves, for those we love, for those we do not love, and for all beings everywhere.

We may want to hate but we can practice love instead, even at the same moment. Two opposing forces can coexist—co-emergent arising—but not for long. Eventually, one will supplant the other. This is how loving-kindness as a practice releases us from our inclination toward hate and retaliation.

Thus the potential for transformation of our dark side lies within us if we practice, that is, act as if we were loving, until it becomes second nature, our real nature after all. This is because our pure inherent goodness *wants* to be manifest and will be successful in clearing away our ignorance and aggression. Our practice of loving-kindness is how we let this happen.

The practice of loving-kindness is in keeping with the moral recommendations of most religions. It affirms the importance of universal and unconditional love, an essential human commitment if we are to survive as a species. It affirms the basic goodness of all people so that we never give up on anyone but include everyone in our circle of love.

We practice loving-kindness when we aspire each day to these four immeasurable blessings for ourselves and others. We do this by aspiring, affirming, or praying, aloud or silently, that the four blessings be granted to ourselves, to those we love, to those with whom we have difficulty, and to all beings everywhere:

Joy: happiness about our own and others' success

Compassion: wanting ourselves and others to be free from pain

Love: wanting ourselves and others to be fulfilled and enlightened

Equanimity: wanting ourselves and others to be stable and serene no matter what the circumstances

A shorter alternative is to practice the same set of aspirations for ourselves and others to have happiness, fulfillment, and enlightenment.

In addition, we are engaging in loving-kindness practice when we greet the considerate actions and words of others toward us with appreciation. When others are not kind or do not like us, the practice is to accept that as a given of life and not to retaliate. Instead, we beam back loving-kindness to them and move out of harm's way. (My book *The Sacred Heart of the World: Restoring Mystical Devotion to Our Spiritual Life* [Paulist, 2007] gives details of this practice.)

> "The line separating good and evil passes not through states, nor between classes, nor between political parties either, but right through every human heart. This line shifts. Inside us, it oscillates with the years. And even within hearts overwhelmed by evil, one small bridgehead of good is retained."
>
> —ALEXANDER SOLZHENITSYN,
> *GULAG ARCHIPELAGO*

Epilogue

The Call to Be Cosmic

*What question was the universe yearning
to have answered when it created me?*

Our personality is an accumulation of our unique experiences. These can contribute to how we grow and how the world grows with us. Sometimes the spiritual seems to be so much about oneness that it diminishes our individuality. In healthy religious consciousness our goal is individuality *and* universality, not the loss of individuality to enter universal consciousness. This fits our evolutionary nature as beings who, as part of a collective, are excited to make a personal donation to a vast, star-studded universe.

A devotion to earth means acting in ways that acknowledge how all is interconnected and yet unique. Indeed, if our origin is from the (most recent) big bang, then diversity arose and keeps arising from oneness. Moreover, from simplicity comes complexity and diversity. If evolution means more and more diversity, then the world is a model for how we can live together in love: honoring one another's differences. Egoic religion does not help us do that but spiritually aware religion can. An adult in faith finds herself there.

Incarnation is an archetype that refers to an appearance of the divine in human form. This was a common theme in ancient religions. A familiar example is belief in the incarnation of God in Jesus or of Vishnu in Krishna. The incarnation archetype shows that a phenomenal reality can include an aspect of divinity, that the manifest and unmanifest are two sides of one reality. Visible and invisible coalesce. All phenomena are embodiments of the whole.

Incarnation shows the fervor of the divine to join, support, and remain present in the human condition, the enthusiasm the divine has for presence among us. Included in the universal meaning of God is just such a connection to humanity, a reliable presence that shares in our life conditions, especially our suffering: "Even though I walk through the darkest valley, I fear no evil; for you are with me" (Ps 23).

In *The Adventure of Consciousness* Sri Aurobindo says that incarnation happens for the same reason that creation happens, so that the divine can reach its full dimensions in the universe: "What, you ask, was the beginning of it all? Existence multiplied itself for sheer delight of being. It plunged into numberless trillions of forms so that it might find itself innumerably."

In the dualistic world of Descartes, meaning and purpose are only in us humans and only we have souls. Nature then is only matter in motion. The rational self is separate from all else and above it all. Humans have consciousness and nothing else does. A planetary spirituality is then impossible and unnecessary.

In the primitive religious view, all is living and in motion. All things are shimmering with sparks of divinity. Our inner life is continuous with it all. There is a soul and sense in all existence, described dramatically and experienced ritually in myth and religion. A planetary spirituality is then possible and certainly necessary.

The book of Deuteronomy says: "I have set before you life and death, blessings and curses. Choose life so that you and your descendants may live" (30:19). We humans need advice like that, given our history, both personally and historically. We are nature's experiment of an unprogrammed species. We have free choice, not only instinct, so we can act against the survival of ourselves as well as of our planet. Unlike all the other animals, we have to be *told* to "choose life." Faith is our positive response and ongoing commitment to the life of the universe: "Where everything began. The world's life. Mine" (James Merrill, "The 'Ring' Cycle").

In the new cosmological view, the universe has a passion for survival and evolution all its own. As we open, it unfolds in us and in all things. We become the operant hands and feet of the divine life in the world. We align ourselves to its evolutionary motion rather than use it for our own acquisitive purposes. Nature brings the presence of the divine, and we are how nature shows this presence in bodily, rational, affective, and spiritual form.

The evolution of the universe has a direction, diversity and complexity, but not an ending target. We are not moving toward an absolute apex-ending of evolution but simply journeying on in an expanding, that is, ever-opening universe. This is like the history of poetry. It is not moving toward a final poem; it is ever opening into new forms and possibilities. A wise "nothing is final" is a commitment to join in the opening. We certainly do this in our small way when we keep revising our personalities—as we do our poems.

Everything is evolving; everything is being renewed. This is a metaphor for our own inner urge—and that of all of nature—toward more and more integration. A faith, religion, or spirituality that insists on fixed formulations or obedient dependency cannot work for beings like us whose "God is marching on." Our journey is not to faraway lands but to the center of ourselves, the core that is the sacred heart of the universe. That center is where the God/Self is, that is, where love, wisdom, and healing are, the tools that build a world of justice, peace, and love.

Some mythic stories tell us that the center is difficult to find; others proclaim that an effortless ease can attain it. Thus a journey to find a gold ring somewhere in Jerusalem requires great effort. The discovery of the gold of the higher Self is as close as one's own heart. In moments in which our love becomes universal and unconditional, our wisdom clear, our healing extending out to the whole world, we are in our highest Self, in what is called God, the gold of the universal Self. This may be what St. Teresa meant when she wrote: "Within us lies something incomparably more precious than what we see outside ourselves."

In addition, since we live as a collective humanity, any journey we undertake individually is the equivalent of that of mythic heroes. Thus our finding the gold of unconditional love in our practice of loving-kindness is no different from Jason's finding the golden fleece or Jacob receiving the angelic blessing. There is only one human journey, and it is to the More of eternity in the Now, the More of sacred space in the Here. The journey was always only to Here Now, though it had names like Ithaca and Timbuktu.

The passage is from ignorance of our wholeness to the enlightening realization that it was in us all along though we sought it elsewhere. We thought it was in an Eden that was lost to us and is now in a faraway heaven. We were forgetting the words of Japanese Buddhist poet Hakuin: "This very moment is eternity, and this very place is the lotus paradise." Thus the essential task in the heroic journey is not finding a map but remembering that there is no need for one. A faith that confirms that is the one that sets us free.

> *"The Age of Nations is past. The task before us now, if we would not perish, is to build the Earth. . . . We have reached a crossroads in human evolution where the only road which leads forward is towards a common passion. . . .*
> *To continue to place our hopes in a social order achieved by external violence would simply amount to our giving up all hope of carrying the Spirit of the Earth to its limits."*
>
> —TEILHARD DE CHARDIN

About the Author

David Richo, Ph.D., M.F.T., teacher and workshop leader, works as a psychotherapist in Santa Barbara and San Francisco, California. He combines Jungian, transpersonal, and mythic perspectives in his work.

Books published by Paulist Press:

How to Be an Adult: A Handbook on Psychological and Spiritual Integration (Paulist Press, 1991)

When Love Meets Fear: How to Become Defense-Less and Resource-Full (Paulist Press, 1997)

The Sacred Heart of the World: Restoring Mystical Devotion to Our Spiritual Life (Paulist Press, 2007)

Books published by other publishers:

Shadow Dance: Liberating the Power and Creativity of Your Dark Side (Shambhala, 1999)

How to Be an Adult in Relationships: The Five Keys to Mindful Loving (Shambhala, 2001)

The Five Things We Cannot Change and the Happiness We Find by Embracing Them (Shambhala, 2005)

Mary Within Us: A Jungian Contemplation of Her Titles and Powers (Human Development Books, 2007)

The Power of Coincidence: How Life Shows Us What We Need to Know (Shambhala, 2007)

Everyday Commitments: Choosing a Life of Love, Realism, and Acceptance (Shambhala, 2007)

When the Past Is Present: Healing the Emotional Wounds That Sabotage Our Relationships (Shambhala, 2008)

Wisdom's Way: Quotations for Contemplation (Human Development Books, 2008)

Making Love Last: How to Sustain Intimacy and Nurture Connection. Set of CDs of a workshop (Shambhala, 2008)

Being True to Life: Poetic Paths to Personal Growth (Shambhala, 2009)

Website for CDs and events: *davericho.com*

green press
INITIATIVE

Paulist Press is committed to preserving ancient forests and natural resources. We elected to print this title on 30% post consumer recycled paper, processed chlorine free. As a result, for this printing, we have saved:

4 Trees (40' tall and 6-8" diameter)
1 Million BTUs of Total Energy
420 Pounds of Greenhouse Gases
2,021 Gallons of Wastewater
123 Pounds of Solid Waste

Paulist Press made this paper choice because our printer, Thomson-Shore, Inc., is a member of Green Press Initiative, a nonprofit program dedicated to supporting authors, publishers, and suppliers in their efforts to reduce their use of fiber obtained from endangered forests.

For more information, visit www.greenpressinitiative.org

Environmental impact estimates were made using the Environmental Defense Paper Calculator. For more information visit: www.papercalculator.org.